HEINEMANN ● ENGLISH ● LANGUAGE ● PRACTICE

H·E·L·P
WITH
WORDS

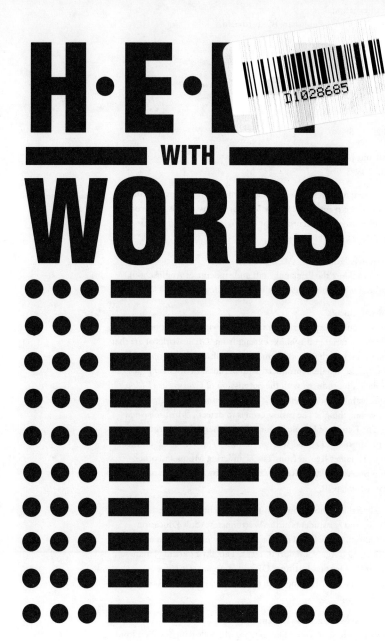

NICK HALL
JOHN SHEPHEARD

HEINEMANN

Heinemann International
A division of Heinemann Publishers (Oxford) Ltd,
Halley Court, Jordan Hill, Oxford, OX2 8EJ

OXFORD LONDON EDINBURGH
MADRID PARIS ATHENS BOLOGNA
MELBOURNE SYDNEY AUCKLAND SINGAPORE TOKYO
IBADAN NAIROBI GABORONE HARARE
PORTSMOUTH (NH)

ISBN 0 435 28117 8

Authors' acknowledgements
We would like to thank the Principal, staff and students of Angloschool,
London, without whose help this book would be the poorer.

Text acknowledgements
The authors and publisher are grateful to the following for their permission
to use copyright material in this book: extract from 'Great works of art that
make men mad' by Jonathan Cooper and Tim Walker, *The European*,
20.9.91, p 48; Minke Whale, reproduced with permission of *Greenpeace Ltd*,
p 83; Planet Earth, reproduced with the permission of *Greenpeace Ltd*, p 92;
'The least successful crime prevention', 'The most noticeable burglar',
'Stealing the wrong thing', 'The easiest crimes to detect', 'Most mis-spelt
name' from The Return of Heroic Failures by Stephen Pile, Reprinted with
permission of *Martin Secker and Warburg Limited*, pp 37, 39, 62; extract
from The Sea, © James Reeves from The Wandering Moon and other
Poems (Puffin Books) by James Reeves. Reprinted by permission of the *The
James Reeves Estate*, p 10.

We would like to thank the following for their help in writing texts in Unit
23: Lucy Taylor and her students at the Westminster Adult Education
Institute (Amharic), Kyaw Swe Tint of the Embassy of the Union of
Myanmar (Burmese), Agapi Tsiakiri (Greek), Tamaki Yokochi (Japanese),
Mark Setton at the Oriental Institute, Oxford (Korean), Dr Irina
Kuzminskaya (Russian), Mr Vongsakul of the Bangkok House Restaurant,
Oxford (Thai).

Photograph and artwork acknowledgements
The authors and publisher would like to thank the following for their kind
permission to reproduce photographs and artwork: All-Sport (UK) Ltd, p 66;
Robert Estall Photographs, p 51; Mary Evans Picture Library, pp 83, 86; Paul
Freestone, p 35; Nick Hall, p 96; The Mansell Collection, p 33; South
American Pictures, p 29; Frank Spooner Pictures Ltd, pp iv, 45.

Illustrations by Barry Atkinson, Satoshi Kambayashi, Jacky Rough,
Shaun Williams
Designed by Helen Hible

Phototypeset in 11/13pt Sabon by Advanced Filmsetters (Glasgow) Ltd
Printed and bound in Great Britain by The Bath Press, Avon.
93 94 95 96 97 98 10 9 8 7 6 5 4 3 2 1

Contents

Introduction

Do you need **Help with Words?**

Are you an intermediate, upper-intermediate or advanced student?

Or are you preparing for the Cambridge First Certificate, the Cambridge Certificate of Advanced English or the Cambridge Proficiency exam?

Do you need help with words?

Did Erno Rubik *invent* or *discover* the famous Rubik Cube? (unit 12)

Can you *steal* or *rob* a bank? (unit 6)

▶ **Help with Words** helps with English words which are similar or confusing:

—some English words are confusing in form and meaning, for example, *lie* and *lay*, or *died, dead, die* and *death*.

—some English words have similar meanings but you need to know when to use which word, for example, *voyage, trip, travel, excursion* and *journey*.

—some English words are 'false friends' which look the same as words in your own language but have different meanings, for example, *control* for French and German learners.

—some English words are 'false friends' which have similar forms and meanings as words in your own language but are not used in exactly the same way, for example, *voyage* for French learners.

How does **Help with Words** help?

▶ **Help with Words** shows you the differences between some of the most commonly confused words. The book includes 25 units, each about a chosen group of words. You can either work through the book or you can look at the Contents page or in the Index to find which unit deals with your particular problem words.

Each unit gives you quick definitions with pronunciations and then gives you a short test:

lose /luːz/: no longer have something and not know where it is
spend /spend/: use, usually time, money or energy

Which verb is always negative in meaning? (unit 5)

▶ **Help with Words** then puts the confusing words into interesting contexts to help you remember the words and so that you can see how the words are used. Often you will want to read the contexts because they are interesting:

> Can you hear anything when you are unconscious? (unit 9)

▶ Next, **Help with Words** checks your pronunciation:

> Does the last *d* in *dressed* sound like the *d* in *do* or the *t* in *to*? (unit 14)

▶ Then **Help with Words** gives useful grammatical information. There is information showing which words come before and after particular words:

> You *steal* things from people.
> You *rob* people or banks of something. (unit 6)

▶ Now **Help with Words** checks and tests the use of the confusing words:

> The following story is true but is the word in *italics* correct?

> After a heart attack, doctors sent Edmund Wilbourne to the hospital mortuary thinking he was dead. Suddenly, he woke up and found himself *laying* on a table. He sat up and the mortuary attendant fainted! (unit 2)

▶ Finally, **Help with Words** gives practice in using the words:

> Complete an interview with famous British athlete, John Regis, to practise using *interesting, interested, exciting, excited, boring, bored*. (unit 20)

▶ There are also five Revision Units which you can do to check that you have understood and remembered what you have learnt. At every step you can check your answers in the Answer Key at the back of the book.

ADVICE TO STUDENTS:

When you do the exercises it is better to use pencil or write the answers on another sheet so you can do the same exercises again. When you reach the Practice section you may like to stop and do it another day as it is good for revision.

borrow, lend 1

Can I borrow an egg?
Yes, I can lend you one.

A CONTEXT

▶ **Look at the questions and then read the text to find the answers.**

a Was 1852 a good time for the customer to borrow money? ....

b Was 1852 a good time for the bank to lend money? ....

1852—A good time to borrow money?

Banks make money because they lend money. When a British bank lent money to business between November 1979 and July 1980, it charged a minimum interest of 17%. But if a bank had lent you money between 1939 and 1951, you would have paid 2%—the lowest ever lending rate. If a business person had borrowed money from the bank in 1852, they also would have paid just 2%.

B DEFINITIONS

▶ **1 Write *lend* or *borrow* next to the correct definition.**

a .... you give something to somebody and later they should give it back

b .... you take something from somebody and later you should give it back

▶ **2 Read the following sentences and answer the questions.**

a 'Can I lend some money to help with the cost of the repairs?' said Dawn.

Is the money Dawn's?...

b 'Can I borrow some money to help with the cost of the repairs?' said Jane.

Is the money Jane's? ....

1

C WHAT COMES AFTER THE VERBS?

▶ 1 Fill in the table. Decide which structures below are possible. Put a tick ✓ in the correct column.

Example: lend something

a lend something somebody

b lend somebody something

c borrow something

d borrow something from somebody

	possible	impossible
	✓	

D PARTS OF THE VERBS

▶ Fill in the parts of the verbs.

infinitive	past simple	past participle
lend /lend/		
borrow /bɒrəʊ/		

E CHECKING

▶ Choose the correct sentence from each pair of sentences.

1 a In the past, some countries borrowed too much money from the World Bank.
  b In the past, the World Bank lent too much money some countries.

2 a 'Friends, Romans, countrymen, borrow me your ears.'
  b 'Friends, Romans, countrymen, lend me your ears.'
    Anthony talking to the crowd in Rome in 'Julius Caesar' by William
    Shakespeare (1564–1616)

3 a Never borrow a stranger money.
  b Never lend money to a stranger.

4 a If you lend to your friend your car, you may lose both your friend and your car.
  b If you lend your friend your car, you may lose both your friend and your car.

5 a Can I borrow you your computer and daisywheel printer?
  b Can I borrow your computer and daisywheel printer?

F TESTING

▶ **Complete the sentences using the words in the box. Remember to use the correct tense of the verbs.**

> borrow   lend   to   from

High finance

1 Brazil has serious problems because it has (a) .... 900 000 million dollars (b)... the World Bank and now cannot pay the money back.

2 London is one of the big banking centres in the world and every day
(a) .... millions of pounds (b) .... poorer countries.

3 The story of Onassis is the classic one of poor boy to riches. When he was 16 years old, he (a) .... a few pounds to buy an old boat. When he was 26, he had a multi-million pound shipping empire. Now people (b) .... thousands of pounds (c) .... the company he started for their own businesses.

G PRACTICE

▶ **1 Write four true sentences using the words in the table. Use one word or phrase from each column in every sentence.**

Students Rich art collectors House buyers Banks	borrow lend	money books paintings	to from	new businesses. libraries. galleries. banks.

a ....

b ....

c ....

d ....

▶ **2 Complete these sentences with a suitable phrase, including *lend* or *borrow*.**

a I haven't got a wedding dress, so ....

b You can have my camera, but don't ....

2 lay, lie 1, lie 2

A CONTEXTS

▶ **Which picture matches which text?**

1   2   3

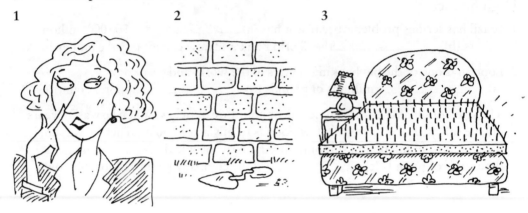

a Two weeks lying in bed?

How long can anyone lie on a bed of nails? Ken Owen set a world record when he lay on such a bed for 300 hours in 1986. In 1969, a man called Silki claimed to have lain on a similar bed of nails for 111 days in São Paolo, Brazil.

b How to tell if someone is lying

Researchers tell us that body language can show if someone has lied to us about something. Common gestures when people are not being honest are rubbing the eyes, scratching the neck below the ear, covering the mouth, and touching the nose. However, an open hand shows truth and honesty.

c World bricklaying record

Tony Gregory of England laid 747 bricks, each weighing 2 kg, in 60 minutes on 18 April 1987.

B DEFINITIONS AND PARTS OF THE VERBS

▶ **Fill in the missing parts of the verbs.**

infinitive	-*ing* form	past simple	past participle	definition
lie				have the body in a horizontal position
lie		lied		say something you know is not true
lay			laid	put in position

C CHECKING

▶ **Read the texts and correct the verbs in *italics* if they are wrong.**

a Admiral Nelson refused to lose a battle. In 1801 in the Battle of Copenhagen, Nelson's commander saw great danger and signalled to stop all action. Nelson put his telescope to his blind eye and said, 'I see no signal. Go on fighting.' Later the battle was won. Was Nelson really *lieing*?

b After a heart attack, doctors sent Edmund Wilbourne to the hospital mortuary thinking he was dead. Suddenly he 'woke up' and found himself *laying* on a table. He sat up and the mortuary attendant fainted!

c Eleven days before Christmas in 1900, the lighthouse on Flannan Isle in the Atlantic was found deserted. Strangest of all was the fact that breakfast things had been *laid* on the table ready for the three lighthouse keepers. The food was untouched.

D TESTING

▶ **1 Complete the sentences using the correct form of *lie* or *lay*.**

a How long did Ken Owen .... on the bed of nails?

b Silki .... on his bed of nails longer than Owen.

c If someone rubs his eyes while he is telling you something, it is quite possible that he

is ....

d How many bricks did Tony Gregory .... ?

▶ **2 Write three sentences using a phrase from each column.**

a	She	lay	about the beach	—it wasn't sandy at all.
b	She	laid	on the beach	on the beach because the sand was wet.
c	She	lied	her towel	and got sunburnt.

a ....

b ....

c ....

E PRACTICE

▶ **1 Complete these sentences with a suitable phrase. Include a different verb from the box in each sentence.**

> lie(1)   lie(2)   lay

a You look really tired, ...

b It's time for lunch, Tim, the plates are over there, ...

c When the police ask you what happened, ...

▶ **2 Using one of the verbs, lie(1), lie(2), or lay, make sentences which mean the same as the sentences given.**

a He never told the truth.

He ....

b She put the knives, forks and glasses on the table.

She ....

c He stayed in bed for an extra hour.

He ....

Lying in bed? What are the two meanings?

6

remember, remind

You remind me of someone but I can't remember who.

A DEFINITIONS

▶ Match the verbs a–d to the sentences 1–4.

a **remember** /rɪˈmembə/ **to do something:**   not forget to do something

b **remember doing something:**   be able to bring back to mind an action from the past

c **remind** /rɪˈmaɪnd/ **somebody to do something:**   tell somebody to do something because they might forget

d **remind somebody of somebody or something:**   make somebody think of somebody or something because they are similar in some way

1 He remembered going to school as a child.
2 She reminds me of her mother.
3 She remembered to lock her car before she came into the house.
4 He reminded me to turn off all the lights before I left.

7

B CONTEXTS

▶ **Read each text and decide if the statement which follows it is true or false.**

a Baby Yogi

Yogananda, the famous Indian yogi, writes in his autobiography that he remembers lying in his bed when he was a baby and listening to his parents talk. He could understand what they were saying. The problem was that he could not talk and take part in the conversation.

Yogananda was different from most babies.   **True/False**

b Perfume of Mum?

Dr George Dodd, working at the University of Warwick in England, has found a natural solution to the problem of stress. He has created a perfume which reminds you of the smell of the fresh, clean skin of your mother when you were a new-born baby. You sniff it four times a day to relieve stress and create feelings of comfort like those experienced when babies are a few hours old in their mother's arms. People sleep better and feel more relaxed.

The perfume smells like the skin of a young baby's mother.   **True/False**

c Do (k)not forget

It was Patrick Smart's wife's birthday the next day and he tied a knot in his handkerchief so that he would remember to buy her a present. Later the next day, he pulled out his handkerchief. 'That's strange,' he thought, 'What's this knot for? I must have tied it to remind me to do something. But what?'

The knot helped Mr Smart.   **True/False**

C PRONUNCIATION

▶ **1 Match the words with the correct stress pattern.**

a remember   i) ☐□□   ii) □☐□   iii) □□☐

b remind   i) ☐□   ii) □☐

▶ **2** *Remind* rhymes with *find*.   **True/False**

D TESTING

▶ **1 Read the sentences. Does the first sentence mean the same as the second sentence?**

a | **remember + to + infinitive** |

She remembered to lock the door. = She remembered first and locked the door second.   **Yes/No**

b | **remember + verb + -ing** |

She remembered locking the door. = She locked the door first and remembered the action later.   **Yes/No**

▶ **2 Read the sentences. If there are mistakes in the *use* of *remind* or *remember*, correct them.**

a This photo remembers me your father; you look exactly the same.
b Remember me to get some petrol before we go back home.
c I remember to take the money but I don't remember spend it.
d Did you remember to put the answerphone on last night?
e Please remember switching on the answerphone tomorrow.

▶ **3 Answer these questions.**

a You want to give someone an instruction, what do you say?
  i) Remember to buy some butter.
  ii) Remember buying some butter.
b You plan to call the electrician but you have a bad memory, what do you say?
  i) Remember to call the electrician.
  ii) Remind me to call the electrician.

▶ **4 Complete the sentences using *remind* or *remember* in the correct form.**

Every time I see a book by Patrick White, the British born Australian novelist, I (a) .... reading one of his famous sayings: 'I forget what I was taught, I only (b) .... what I've learnt.' It (c) .... me of my time at school.

E PRACTICE

▶ **1 Write four sentences using the words in the box. Use each word at least once.**

reminded	to	he	of	visiting	me
my	remembered	visit	friend		

Example: *He remembered me.*

a ....

b ....

c ....

d ....

▶ **2 Summarise the texts using *remind* or *remember*.**

a 'Dave, don't forget to water the plants when I'm away,' said Jenny.

Jenny ....

b **Detective:** Did you see anyone?
Witness: Yes, wait a minute, there was a man. Yes, near the station. He came out and seemed to be waiting for something.

The witness ....

c Eddie was cooking his breakfast. He broke two eggs into the frying pan and put it on the gas cooker. Suddenly, the phone rang. It was his mother. 'Come quickly!' she said. There was some kind of problem. So Eddie rushed out and drove off in his car. As he arrived at his mother's house, he thought, 'Oh no! The eggs!'

Eddie ....

d The Sea

The sea is a hungry dog,
Giant and grey ...   James Reeves

The sea ....

say, tell

4

A CONTEXT

▶ **Look at the question and then read the text to find the answer.**

Which speaker clearly understood my question? ....

My Chinese isn't very good. When I was in Beijing, I asked the way to the airport.
The first person said nothing and walked away.
The second person said to me that he didn't have a light.
The third person said thank you to me.
The fourth person told me the story of his life.
The fifth person told me that it was straight on.

B WHAT COMES AFTER THE VERBS?

▶ **1 Look at the text above and decide which is correct, *a* or *b*.**

a

say	somebody	something
tell	somebody	something

b

say	something	(to somebody)
say	to somebody	that ...
tell	somebody	something

NOTE: You can *tell (somebody) a story, a lie, a joke, the truth. Somebody* is not
necessary when you use these four nouns.

▶ **2 One sentence is correct—which one?** ....

a Can you *tell to me the time?*   d Can you *tell the time to me?*
b Can you *say to me the time?*   e Can you *tell me the time?*
c Can you *say me the time?*

11

C PRONUNCIATION

said /sɛd/   Does *said* rhyme with *paid* or *red*? ....

D WHAT CAN COME AFTER THE VERBS?

It is **possible** to use
say with:

these nouns	*-thing* words	these words
the same	something	much
the opposite	everything	(very) little
the obvious	nothing	a lot
	anything	it
	some good things	that

but it is **impossible** to use
tell with: **say** with:

single conversation words, for example,
goodbye
hello
yes
no
sorry

most nouns, for example,
the problem
the answer
your age
the time
a lie
a story
etc

E CHECKING

► **There are mistakes in nine of these sentences. Find the mistakes and correct them.**

a   Somebody said me that you would come. *[told me]*

b   I never tell anybody that I am divorced, that I have seventeen children and that I am an alcoholic.

c   Can you say to me the answer?

d   Can you say me the answer? *[tell me]*

e   They said to come back later.

f   Can you tell to me the answer?

g   He told that there were no answers to me. *[me]*

h   Somebody told that you were here. *[me]*

i   He said something about elephants to me. *[told me]*

j   Can you say the answer to me? *[tell me]*

k   He said goodbye to everybody.

l   He told me goodbye. *[said ... to me]*

m   Sometimes it is better to tell a lie than to tell the truth.

n   He said a long story. *[told]*

✗ F TESTING

▶ Write six sentences using the words in the box. Start every sentence with *Don't* or *He*—shown by the tints. You can go in *all* directions but you cannot jump a square. At least ten sentences are possible.

to	write	tell	**Don't**	say
mother	to	him	the	anything
his	nothing	that	truth	please
to	said	a	he	French
sorry	**He**	lot	was	a

Examples: Don't tell him the truth.   He said sorry.

1 ....
2 ....
3 ....
4 ....
5 ....
6 ....

G PRACTICE

▶ Rewrite the following sentences so that they mean the same. You must use *say* or *tell* in each sentence.

a I lied.

I *did not tell the truth.*

b I didn't speak.

I *did not say anything.*

c I ordered him to do it again.

I *told him to do it again.*

d In his opinion the new system is no good.

He *said that the new system is no good.*

e I repeated the whole message to him.

I *told him the whole message again.*

f I told him something about the new company.

I *said to him something about the new company*

13

5 lose, miss, pass, spend, waste

A DEFINITIONS

▶ **1 Read the definitions and decide which three verbs are always negative in meaning.**

a ....   b ....   c ....

miss /mɪs/:
i) feel unhappy because you no longer have something you like or do something you like; or because someone you like is no longer with you
Example: *Sarah missed her husband when he went away on business.*
ii) fail to do something you intended; fail to hit, catch, find, meet, or see someone or something
Example: *I missed him at the station when I went to meet him. I arrived late and missed the start of the film. I kicked the ball badly and missed the goal.*

lose /luːz/:
no longer have something and not know where it is
Example: *I lost my luggage at the airport because I wrote the wrong address on it.*

waste /weɪst/:
use wrongly, or use too much of something, usually time, money, or energy
Example: *She wastes lots of money on clothes she doesn't need.*

spend /spend/:
use, usually time, money or energy
Example: *We often spend quite a lot of time, money, and energy organising big parties.*

pass /pɑːs/:
i) occupy time—in the expression *pass the time*
Example: *It was a wet day and we passed the time playing card games.*
ii) be successful in an examination
Example: *She passed all her school exams and was accepted for university.*

▶ **2 Fill in the table. Put a tick ✓ under the words which can complete the sentences. It may be possible to tick more than one column.**

	an absent friend.	the first flight to Rome.	your time watching TV if you're tired.	your cheque book in the street.	your driving test if you're careful.
Example:					
You can miss	✓	✓			
a You can lose					
b You can waste					
c You can spend					
d You can pass					

B CONTEXT

▶ **Read the text and find three disadvantages of driving to work.**

A better way of passing the time of day

Today, in a lot of American cities many motorists spend up to two hours in their cars every morning travelling to work. Most of that time is simply wasted sitting in traffic jams. Instead of gaining time and freedom by having a car, drivers are now losing everything they hoped to gain as they are now prisoners in their own cars. Perhaps if they started to use public transport they would not miss the 'luxury' of having a car and they would also not miss so many of their important business appointments.

The three disadvantages of driving to work are:

a ....

b ....

c ....

C PRONUNCIATION

Does *lose* rhyme with *news* or *loose*? ....

15

D CHECKING

▶ **Read the text and correct any of the words in *italics* which are wrong.**

1 Why do so many rich people *pass* their time in casinos? All they do is *spend* a lot of money and *lose* their time drinking. Surely they could *waste* their time in a more enjoyable and useful way. They could *pass* the time helping poorer people live more comfortably. They need to live and suffer in a real world. They need to experience

5 not having enough money just in small ways, like *losing* the last train at night and having to walk home because they cannot pay for a taxi. The best experience in life is to *miss* something and then have to fight to get it back.

E TESTING

▶ **Decide which of the five verbs in *italics* can be used to complete each sentence. More than one verb may be correct.**

a It was late and I had *missed/passed/lost/spent/wasted* the last ferry across the Bosphorus.

b I went to the covered market in Istanbul and I *missed/passed/lost/spent/wasted* a lot of money.

c I went to the famous Topkapi Palace where the sultans used to live and *missed/ passed/lost/spent/wasted* a great day looking at all the treasures from the Ottoman Empire.

d I wanted to see the rooms where the harem lived but unfortunately I *missed/passed/ lost/spent/wasted* them.

e I wonder how many Turkish people *miss/pass/lose/spend/waste* the old way of life and rich tradition of the sultans.

F PRACTICE

▶ **Complete these sentences with a suitable phrase. Include a different verb from the box in each sentence.**

miss miss lose spend waste

a There is a bus that visits all the caves in Cappadocia but it leaves at six in the morning so don't ....

b There are many caves and some of them have frescoes but the caves are very big and dark. Be careful with your camera and don't ....

c Some of the shops have some wonderful Ottoman antiques so don't go crazy and ....

d The sunset near Göreme is sensational so don't ....

e The midday sun can be very hot and you will get thirsty and dirty so take a bottle of water. Only use a little at a time and don't ....

Revision A
────── *units 1–5* ──────

1 borrow, lend (unit 1)

A MEANING

▶ **Read the sentences and answer the questions.**

a William borrowed a camera from Brian.

Who does the camera belong to? ....

b Jenny lent Dave a book.

Who does the book belong to? ....

c Eric had £20. He borrowed £5 and then lent a friend £10.

How much money has Eric got now? ....

B STRUCTURE

▶ **Put the words into the table in the correct order. Use each of the following words once.**

~~something~~ something something ~~someone~~ someone someone to from

a	lend	.....*someone*.....	.....*something*.....
b	lend	....	....	....
c	borrow	....	....	....

C USE

▶ **Complete the sentence in two ways using *lend* and *borrow*.**

Emma: Dad, I need £500 to buy a second-hand car. Can ...

a Can ....

b Can ....

17

2 lay, lie 1, lie 2, remember, remind, say, tell
(units 2, 3, 4)

▶ **Read the clues and complete the crossword.**

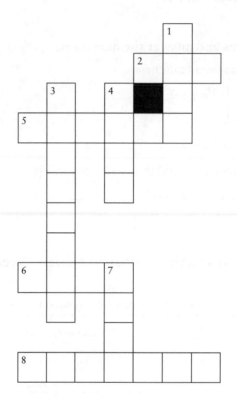

Across

2 Tim was in bed when he felt a scorpion on his arm.
He .... completely still and did not dare to move.

5 To tell somebody to do something so they do not forget.

6 Can you .... me what time the party starts?

8 Do you remember .... your first book at school?

Down

1 I .... no and I meant it!

3 .... to post the letter.

4 He .... about his age to get the job.

7 They .... the injured player on the grass.

3 lose, miss, pass, spend, waste (unit 5)

A MEANING

▶ **1 Read the sentences and answer the questions.**

a He's missing his wife.

   i) Is she with him now? ....

   ii) Was she with him before? ....

   iii) Does he want her to be with him now? ....

b He missed his wife at the station.

   i) Did he go to the station? ....

   ii) Did he meet her? ....

c He wasted his time learning English.

   i) Did he study English? ....

   ii) Was it a good idea? ....

d She spent all her money on a new jacket.

   i) Has she bought a new jacket? ....

   ii) Does she have any money left? ....

e She was in prison for a year and passed the time learning English.

   i) Did she waste her time? ....

   ii) Did she study English? ....

   iii) Which verb can replace *passed* without changing the meaning,
      spent/lost/wasted? ....

f He didn't pass his English examination.

   i) Did he take the examination? ....

   ii) Was he successful? ....

▶ **2 Match the answers to the questions.**

a How did you lose your money?   I bought my wife a present.

b How did you waste your money?   I bought a theatre ticket and was too ill to go.

c How did you spend your money?   I left it in a bag on the train.

B USE

▶ **Rewrite the sentences below using the verbs in the box. Do not change the meaning of the sentences.**

waste   lose   pass   spend   miss

a He's sad because he loves gardening and now he lives in a flat.

He ....

b She got to the station at 6.05 but the 6 o'clock train had already gone.

She ....

c He had a free afternoon and so he decided to go to the zoo. It took two hours for him to get there and it was shut.

He ....

d When she has any free time, she goes to the cinema.

She ....

e He had an hour to wait for the next bus so he bought a newspaper and read it.

He ....

f They gave her a spelling test and she got them all right.

She ....

g She took off her ring to wash her hands. When she had finished she couldn't find it.

She ....

break in, break into, burgle, mug, rob, steal

A WHAT ARE THE DIFFERENCES?

▶ **1 Read the explanations and examples, and then fill in the table.**

steal /stiːl/: take something illegally, usually secretly
Example: *Somebody stole my bicycle in the middle of the night.*

rob /rɒb/: take from a person or a place sometimes with violence. It often involves large amounts of money, gold, etc and is often connected with banks and institutions.
Example: *They robbed the bank in the High Street and ran off with £100 000. I was robbed as I came out of the bank; they took my wallet.*

mug /mʌg/: attack someone on the street or in a public place and take something from them, usually small amounts of money, jewellery, etc. You can't be mugged inside a building.
Example: *A young man mugged me at the bus stop in broad daylight. He took my briefcase.*

break in /breɪk/: enter a building or vehicle with force. *Break in* does not have an
break into object. *Break into* needs an object.
Example: *Somebody broke in when we were on holiday. Somebody broke into our flat when we were out. They didn't take anything valuable.*

burgle /bɜgəl/: enter a building with force and take things illegally, often from a house
Example: *Our house was burgled last night. They came in through the bathroom window. They took my new camera.*

▶ Now fill in the table. Put a tick √ in the column which shows what kind of object can follow the verb. It may be possible to tick more than one column.

Example:	direct object possible	things	people	buildings	vehicles
steal	√	√			√
a mug			√		
b rob					
c burgle				√	
d break in					√
e break into				√	√

▶ **2 Complete the sentences using each word in the box once only.**

thief   robber   mugger   burglar

a A ......*mugger*...... is a person who attacks you in the street and takes your valuable things by force.

b A ......*thief*...... is a person who steals your things, often without your knowing.

c A ......*robber*...... is a person who steals a lot of money from people anywhere and often has a gun.

d A ......*burglar*...... is a person who either uses a special key, an open door or breaks a window to get into a building so he can steal things.

B CONTEXT

▶ Read the text and decide whether most crimes are against people or property.

Every year about 1 500 000 cars are broken into or stolen in the UK – that's one every 20 seconds. The number of houses broken into or burgled is about 600 000 and 90% of these cases are because windows or doors are not locked. Several banks are robbed and dozens of people are mugged every day.

C WHAT COMES AFTER THE VERB?

GENERAL RULES

steal	things	from	people/places
rob	people or banks	of	something
mug	people		
burgle	a building (not a bank)		
break into	a building/vehicle		
break in			

WARNING: *Break in* is an intransitive verb so it cannot have a direct object.

D CHECKING

▶ Read the texts and change any of the words in *italics* which are incorrect.

a Clever criminals do not ~~*steal*~~ *rob* banks, they do not *steal* people's money, they do not *rob* people, they do not *burgle* houses, they do not even *mug* people, they simply *mug* ~~*rob*~~ other successful criminals.

b **A:** Did they ~~*rob*~~ *steal* your car?
   B: No, they only *broke into* it and *stole* a few maps.

22

E TESTING

▶ **1 Which words and phrases can you use to complete these sentences? Fill in the correct numbers.**

a 6 7 10   b 2 3 ... ...   c 8   d 1   e 3 8 9   f 4

a	You can steal	1	someone in the street.
b	You can rob	2	people of their jewellery.
c	You can burgle	3	a bank.
d	You can mug	4	an old lady in her house.
e	You can break into	5	someone in a restaurant.
f	You can break in	6	a handbag.
		7	top secret information from the government.
		8	a house.
		9	and photograph documents, and leave them in the safe.
		10	a car.

F PRACTICE

▶ **Write a summary of the following articles using about ten words. Include a different verb from the box in each summary.**

> burgle   break into   mug   steal   rob

a On 26 November 1983, six masked men removed 6 800 bars of gold and platinum in 76 boxes together with diamonds and travellers' cheques worth £26 369 778 from the Brinks–Mat company at Heathrow Airport.

Summary: ....

b Criminals entered the villa of Prince Abdel Aziz Bin Ahmed Al-Thani near Cannes, France on 24 July 1980. Jewels valued at $16 000 000 were missing the next day.

Summary: ....

c The 15-year-old attacked at around 9 pm on January 12, getting away with just 25 pence in cash when he attacked a 35-year-old East Croydon lady. The victim was attacked from behind, pushed to the ground and her handbag was snatched from her. She was badly shaken but escaped with only minor cuts and bruises.

Summary: ....

d Last year masked men in Rio de Janeiro ran out of a bank with no money and when they looked for their escape car it had gone.

Summary: ....

e The thief was surprised to find a very friendly guard dog in the large empty villa. He immediately filled his sack with many valuable things from the house and went to the front door. He started to laugh at the stupid dog but then, every time he tried to leave the house, the dog attacked him.

Summary: ....

7 fit, match, suit

A DEFINITIONS

▶ **Read the definitions then match the sentences to the pictures.**

fit /fɪt/:   be the correct size and shape
match /mætʃ/: combine well with or be the same as, often used of colours, styles, shapes, personalities, movements
suit /suːt/:   make you feel or look good

a Her shoes don't fit.
b Her shoes don't match.
c Her shoes don't suit her.

B CONTEXT

▶ **1 Read the text and match the body types with the pictures.**

1   2   3

It is important that our clothes fit our bodies but it is also important that we feel our personalities 'fit' our bodies. People can be divided into three basic types and the description of most people will match one of the following. When we choose a partner we usually choose somebody who suits our particular type.

Ectomorph: a type of person with a body characterised by thinness, weakness and a lack of weight. They are usually intellectual, shy and alert.

Endomorph: a type of person with a body characterised by roundness, fatness and heaviness. They are usually easy-going, relaxed and love life.

Mesomorph: a type of person with a muscular body and a strong bone structure. They are usually energetic, dominant and like meeting people.

▶ **2 Decide if the statements are true or false.**

a According to the text, clothes should be the right size for us.   **True/False**
b Most people will find their type described in the text.   **True/False**
c The author says choosing a partner means finding someone who makes you feel good.   **True/False**

C PRONUNCIATION

Does *suit* rhyme with *sweet* or *boot*? ....

D WHAT COMES AFTER THE VERB?

GENERAL RULES

fit	
fit	somebody or something
match	
match	somebody or something
suit	somebody or something

WARNING: *Suit* needs an object.

You cannot use prepositions, such as *with*, directly after these verbs.

E CHECKING

▶ **Look at the sentences and change any of the words in *italics* which are incorrect.**

a The fingerprints of the gardener and those found on the gun do not *fit*.
b The bullet found in the dead man does not *match* the neighbour's gun.
c The cook cannot be the murderer because the police description does not *suit* him.

F TESTING

▶ **Decide which of the three verbs in *italics* can be used to complete these sentences.**

a Did you know that the colours of the eyes of cats from around Lake Van in Turkey never *suit/match/fit* because one is blue and the other is yellow?
b One man's meat is another man's poison (an English proverb). This means that something might *suit/match/fit* one person but it may make somebody else feel terrible.
c Frustration is that feeling you have when the last piece of a jigsaw puzzle does not *suit/match/fit*.

G PRACTICE

▶ Write three sentences about the picture. Include a different verb from the box in each sentence.

suit   match   fit

a ....

b ....

c ....

8 conduct, drive, get, go, ride, take, travel

A WHAT ARE THE DIFFERENCES?

▶ Read the explanations and then fill in the table below.

drive /draɪv/: control and guide any vehicle
WARNING: You *fly a plane, sail a boat* and *steer a ship or spaceship*—you **cannot** drive them.

ride /raɪd/: sit on and control an animal, bicycle or motorbike

go /gəʊ/
travel /ˈtrævl/ **on**: use public transport

go/travel in: use private transport

go/travel by: use all transport. The phrase never has an article (*a* or *the*).
Example: *I went to town by bus.*
NOTE: *Travel* is a more formal verb than *go*.

take /teɪk/: use public or private transport
Example: *We took the bus to Portsmouth.*

get /get/: use public transport
Example: *Let's get the underground.*
NOTE: *Take* and *get* are informal verbs.

WARNING: *Conduct* means *lead* or *guide*, for example, *conduct a meeting, conduct an orchestra*. Unlike some European languages, it does **not** mean drive and a conductor is not a driver, he/she only sells tickets.

▶ Decide which verbs can be used for public transport and which for private transport. Put a tick ✓ in the correct column or columns. Remember, some verbs can be used for both.

	public	private
Example: drive	✓	✓
a ride		
b go/travel in		
c go/travel on		
d go/travel by		
e take		
f get		

B CONTEXTS

▶ **Match the types of transport with the descriptions.**

> cable car   BMW motorcycle   taxi   tram
> ~~the longest limousine in the world~~   hovercraft
> private car

Example: It has two televisions, a video recorder, three telephones, a fridge, a
sundeck and a jacuzzi. It is twenty-three metres long, it weighs seven and a
half tons and twenty people can travel in it. If you want to drive it, you will
have to spend $200 000 to buy it.

It's *the longest limousine in the world.*

a Let's go by . . ., what do you call it? It runs along rails on the street. The Americans
call it a streetcar. In San Francisco, it has a conductor and a driver.

It's a ....

b The Royal Family's Special Escort Group always ride them. They travel on them in
front of the Queen to clear the traffic and to protect her. They can do 200 kph.

It's a ....

c If you want to visit the top of Sugar Loaf mountain in Rio de Janeiro you have to go
on it, it is almost like flying.

It's a ....

d I always go in it to work because I can decide when to go, how to go and when to
come back home. I can also take passengers if I want to.

It's a ....

e You can take one or get one in the street or from a rank where there are usually a
lot waiting, but they are expensive.

It's a ....

f It is fast and comfortable. It is unusual because it looks like a boat but it feels like a
plane as it sits above the water. I always travel on it across Sydney Harbour.

It's a ....

C PRONUNCIATION

a Does the *i* in *ride* and *drive* have the same pronunciation as the *i* in *fight* or the *ee* in *feet*? ....

b Match the word with the correct stress pattern.

travel   i) ☐☐   ii) ☐☐

D WHEN TO USE THE VERBS

GENERAL RULES

go/travel on	is used for public transport
go/travel in	is used for private transport
go/travel by	is used for both public and private transport

WARNING: A taxi is public before you hire it, so you can *get* a taxi; but it is private after you hire it, so you can *go in* a taxi, but you cannot *go on* a taxi.

E CHECKING

▶ **Look at the text and correct any of the words in *italics* which are wrong.**

1 The best way of seeing Marrakesh, an old city in Morocco, is to *go on a taxi*. Personally I like to *go by public transport* because it is a good way to meet people. It is difficult to *drive a bus* because the names are written
5 in Arabic. The souk, or market, is one of the oldest in the world but you cannot *take a car* there because the streets are too narrow. However you will see people *travelling by the donkey* or *driving a bike*. Unfortunately you cannot *get the tube* because there is none.

F TESTING

▶ **Put these forms of transport into the correct box or boxes.**

> a donkey   donkey   the tube*
> tube   a taxi   taxi   a car   car   the coach
> coach   a plane   plane   the ferry   ferry

*tube = subway, in the USA

It is possible to:

Example:	drive	*a taxi*	*a car*	*the coach*
a	ride			
b	go/travel on			
c	go/travel in			
d	go/travel by			
e	take			
f	get			

G PRACTICE

▶ **Complete these sentences with a suitable word or phrase. Include a different verb from the box in each sentence. Sometimes more than one answer is possible.**

> drive   ride   go   travel   take   get

How do you get to work?

a If you live near a train station, you will probably ....

b If you live in Beijing (Peking), you will probably ....

c If you are a chauffeur, you will probably ....

d If you are in a hurry and have enough money, you will probably ....

....

e If you have to be in Paris or Tokyo by tomorrow, you will probably ....

....

f If you live on a farm without roads, you will probably ....

9 hear, listen, listen to

A WHAT'S THE DIFFERENCE?

▶ **Read the explanation and then answer the questions below.**

The difference between *listen* and *hear* is that
listen /lɪsn/: is something you choose to do or something you can control
hear /hɪə/: is something you don't choose to do or something you have no control
over

▶ **1 Match the questions and answers.**

a What did you hear?   My favourite cassette for half and hour.
b What did you listen to?   A sudden noise.

▶ **2 Which of these two sentences is not logical?**

a I heard the music but I didn't listen to it.
b I listened to the music but I didn't hear it.

B CONTEXT

▶ **Look at the question and then read the text to find the answer.**

Can people *hear* when they are unconscious? ....

Joyce Mills from Hobart, Australia, was listening to her car radio on her way home from work one afternoon when she hit a kangaroo and was knocked out. When the ambulance men arrived, one of them said to the other, 'I think she is going to die.' Obviously he didn't think Joyce could hear the conversation. She was taken to hospital and remained unconscious for a couple of days. Soon after she had regained consciousness, the same ambulance driver came into her ward. She had never met him or seen him before but when she heard his voice, she suddenly turned round and said to him, 'Listen! You were wrong—I didn't die.'

C PRONUNCIATION

a Which letter is silent in *listen*? ....

b Does *hear* rhyme with *her, hair* or *near*? ....

D WHAT COMES AFTER THE VERB?

GENERAL RULES

listen		
listen	to	somebody or something
hear		
hear		somebody or something

WARNING: You need the preposition *to* after *listen*, ~~listen somebody or something~~ is
wrong.

E CHECKING

▶ **There are three mistakes in the *use* of *listen* and *hear* in these sentences.**
Find the mistakes and correct them.

a Didn't you *hear* the cuckoo calling in the woods below?

b I'm sorry, I wasn't *hearing*.

c *Listen!* Can you *hear* the nightingale singing?

d Yes! It's the most beautiful birdsong I have ever *listened*.

e *Listen* the sound of the birds in the trees.

f I'm *listening* but I can only *hear* the wind in the trees.

a nightingale

F TESTING

▶ **Write four logical sentences. Use a phrase or word from each column in**
every sentence.

I can't Please	listen hear listen to	her voice carefully	—it's important. —it's too quiet. —it's wonderful. —it's so awful.

a ....

b ....

c ....

d ....

G PRACTICE

▶ **Complete the following sentences with a suitable word or phrase. Each sentence must include either *listen* or *hear* in the correct form.**

a Deaf people ....

b Impatient people ....

c Men fall in love with their eyes but women fall in love with their ears, because the important thing is not what they see, but what they ....

d We old people can teach young people so much. The problem is they never ....

e Young people go to discos with loud music, have noisy walkmen and always turn up their stereos too high, so when they are older they won't be able to ....

f There was a strange noise a minute ago. Be quiet and ....

g Heavy metal music? I never ....

look, look at, see, watch

A DEFINITIONS

▶ **Read the definitions and then match the questions and answers.**

look /lʊk/: focus your eyes on something or someone
look at Example: *I can't look now. Look at the river, the water is very high.*
watch /wɒtʃ/: focus your eyes on something or someone for a period of time and study any movement carefully
Example: *Watch the river, the water is about to come over its banks.*
see /siː/: use one of the five senses, general verb to talk about ability
Example: *Can you see the river behind the trees?*

a Did you look at his tie?   It was his birthday present. (b)
b Did you see his tie?   It was moving—he's a magician. (c)
c Did you watch his tie?   It had an unusual design. (a)

B CONTEXT

▶ **Look at the question and then read the text to find the answer.**

How can you know from somebody's eyes if they like you?

If somebody likes you, his pupils will   become larger.

MAN WATCHING

People's eyes tell us a lot about their feelings towards us. When we speak to somebody we do not consciously look at their pupils, but this part of their eyes can tell us a lot. Next time you are speaking to somebody, look carefully, you will be surprised at what you will see, because the size of their pupils will slowly change. Watch them as they either get bigger or get smaller and then you will see their true feelings. If their pupils become larger, it means they like you, but if they become smaller, then it means they do not think you are a very nice person.

C WHAT COMES AFTER THE VERB?

GENERAL RULES

look		
look	at	something or somebody
see		
see		something or somebody
watch		
watch		something or somebody

D CHECKING

▶ **Look at the sentences and correct any of the words in *italics* which are wrong.**

a I *watched* the sun go down and the moon come up.

b I *looked* but I didn't see the moon hiding behind the tree.

✓ c If you *look the face* of Leonardo da Vinci's famous painting—the Mona Lisa—you will *see* her smile. *(at)*

d *Look!* If you *watch* this part of the video about the Mona Lisa, you will *see* something very interesting about the distance between her eyes and her mouth.

✓ e *Look the video,* it's broken. *(at)*

f *Look!* The video is broken.

g Don't *see*! I don't like people *looking at me* when I'm dancing. *watch*

E TESTING

▶ **Match the questions and answers.**

a Can you see the TV?   Oh no! It's scratched. (c)

b Can you watch TV?   Oh no! Somebody has stolen it. (a)

c Look at the TV!   Yes, but only for an hour. (b)

F PRACTICE

▶ **Complete each sentence with a different word or phrase.**

look   look at   watch   see

a Rembrandt is famous for his clever contrast of light and dark areas in his paintings but because they are quite old, some areas are so dark you *cannot see them clearly.*

b Modern art, such as expressionism, can be very difficult to understand. You may not know what the painter wants to express, even if you *look carefully*.

c The problem with many art galleries is that there is too much to see. You must be selective, otherwise by the time you get to the end of the exhibition you will be so tired you won't want to *look at* anymore paintings.

d Personally I find the people in art galleries more interesting than the paintings. Their expressions can be fascinating to *watch*.

Revision B

units 6–10

1 break in, break into, burgle, mug, steal, rob (unit 6)

A USE

▶ Read these true stories and complete the sentences with one of the verbs above in the correct tense. Use all the verbs at least once.

a
Two policemen were parked outside the garage of Colin Baggs, a suspected car thief. They had let their windows steam up and were waiting to see what he would do. After a long wait when nothing happened, they decided to drive away. However, before they had time to start their car, Mr Baggs .... their vehicle.

b
An American, Homer Lawyer, had decided to .... a bank in Miami. He gave the cashier a note asking for cash and then ran off with a sack full of money. It was the bank manager who noticed later that Mr Lawyer had written his name and address on the back of the note.

c
Kenneth Beverley was .... an office in Cardiff, Wales, when he knocked over a dictating machine, which switched itself on. Later he was arrested when police recognised his voice on the tape.

d
Two teenagers .... a grocery shop in Yeovil, England, in April 1984. They found what they thought was the cash-box, pulled it from the wall, and ran into the street. Suddenly the box started to make a noise which they could not stop. They had .... the burglar alarm.

e
A doctor was walking through a street in Brisbane, Australia, when he saw a man trying to .... an old lady who was shouting for help. He ran towards the man and grabbed his shoulders. Suddenly the director of the television film stepped forward to protect the actor.

f
In February 1981, a young Soviet burglar found an empty flat at Baku on the Caspian Sea. The owners were away on holiday. He .... and feeling very tired, had a hot bath, and then drank a few vodkas. Finally he decided to play the piano and started to sing in a very loud voice. The police arrived after the neighbours complained about the noise.

2 fit, match, suit (unit 7)

A MEANING

▶ **Match the answers to the questions.**

a Do the shoes fit you?   No, one's a darker green than the other.
b Do the shoes match?   No, green looks terrible on me.
c Do the shoes suit you?   No, they're too big.

3 conduct, drive, get, go, ride, take, travel (unit 8)

A MEANING

▶ **Read the sentences and answer the questions.**

a He's driving to the office where he works. Is he going by car, train, or taxi?

....

b He's conducting. Is he in a bus or a concert hall? ....

B STRUCTURE

▶ **1 One phrase can be used to complete the sentence. Choose the *correct* phrase.**

a She went to work i) by bus.
                    ii) by the bus.
                    iii) with the bus.
b Why don't we go to Rome i) in fast train?
                          ii) by the fast train?
                          iii) on the fast train?
c She went to work i) on the car.
                    ii) in the car.
                    iii) in car.

▶ **2 Two phrases can be used to complete the sentence. Find the *incorrect* phrase.**

a Let's i) get the train to Barcelona.
         ii) take the train to Barcelona.
         iii) travel the train to Barcelona.
b Have you ever i) ridden a bike?
                 ii) ridden a camel?
                 iii) ridden the London underground?
c Would you like to i) drive a plane?
                     ii) drive a racing car?
                     iii) drive a tank?

C USE

▶ **Read the texts and complete the sentences with a word from the box in the correct form. Sometimes more than one answer is possible.**

> drive travel ride go conduct get take

a **Steve:** How am I going to get to school tomorrow?
Anne: Why don't you .... by bike?
Steve: I can't, my tyres are flat.

b Mrs Helen Ireland from California, USA, failed her driving test in the first minute. She did this by mistaking the accelerator pedal for the brake pedal and .... the car straight through the wall of the Driving Test Centre.

c A bank robber in Malta rushed out of the Bank of Valeta and across the road. He had decided to .... a bus. After 15 minutes with no bus in sight, he was arrested by a passing policeman who saw the 3000 new banknotes he was holding to his chest.

d In the 1980s, a Dutch publisher left his seventh party in three hours at the Frankfurt Book Fair in Germany and decided to .... a taxi to his hotel. Next morning he woke up outside his own house in Amsterdam back in Holland. He had shown the driver the wrong card.

4 hear, listen, listen to (unit 9)

▶ **1 Put the words in the right order to make a sentence about the world record for a radio programme.**

| was | to | the sound of | a boxing match | switched on their radios |

| but at first all they were able | an electric storm. | ~~In June 1950,~~ |

| to hear | 30 million adults | to listen |

In June 1950, ...

....

▶ **2 In 1906, Professor Fessenden tried to make the first radio broadcast in Massachusetts, USA. It contained speech and music. Write the short conversation between him and his colleague in the correct order.**

| 'Yes.' | hear | Now listen | can you | to | anything?' |

| ~~'Listen,~~ | Handel's music.' | 'Good. |

'Listen, ...

....

5 look, look at, see, watch (unit 10)

▶ Write four logical sentences using a phrase or word from each column.

Can you	look look at see watch	anything in the dark? the sun without hurting your eyes? the race on TV at 3 o'clock? and try to find my socks?

a ....

b ....

c ....

d ....

come, go

11

A DEFINITIONS

▶ **Read the definitions and then complete the two sentences below using** *coming* **or** *going*.

come /kʌm/:   move to where the speaker or the listener is

go /gəʊ/:   move to a place where neither the speaker nor the listener is

Gianni and Carlo are brothers. They are Italian students in London. Their sister Maria is at home in Rome.

a

> I'm looking forward to _____ home tomorrow.

b

> I'm looking forward to _____ home tomorrow.

B CONTEXTS

▶ **1 Read the texts and put a tick ✓ in the column if the speaker and/or listener is at the prison. It may be possible to tick both or neither column.**

	Is the speaker at the prison?	Is the listener at the prison?
Nelson Mandela Free Today		
a Winnie Mandela speaking to journalists in South Africa in 1990: 'When I go to the prison to meet my husband, I'll be the happiest person in the world.'		
b Winnie Mandela on the phone speaking to her husband: 'When I come to the prison to meet you, the whole world will want to watch us.'		
c Nelson Mandela on the phone in prison talking to his wife. 'What time are you coming to see me tomorrow?'		
d Nelson Mandela speaking to a friend in prison: 'I can't believe it, my wife is coming to collect me from prison tomorrow.'		

▶ **2 Decide if this statement is true or false.**

Go is used when someone or something moves to a place where neither the speaker nor the listener is. *Come* is used for all other situations.   **True/False**

C PRONUNCIATION

a Which words have the same vowel sound as *come—home, some, bomb, run* or *done*? ....

b Which words have the same vowel sound as *go—do, no, so* or *lot*?

....

D WHAT COMES AFTER THE VERB?

GENERAL RULES

go/come	to a place Example: *We went to the shop.*
go/come	here/there/home/abroad Example: *We went there. They came home.*

WARNING: Remember that *come/go* is followed by *to* when the next word is a place except when the next word is *here/there/home/abroad*.

E CHECKING

▶ **Read the texts and decide if the statements below are true or false.**

a Come to the Kremlin
'When you come back to the Kremlin the President will be here to meet you.'
The speaker and the listener are not at the Kremlin.   **True/False**

b Go to the White House
'If you go to the White House, the President will be there to meet you.'
The speaker and the listener are at the White House.   **True/False**

F TESTING

▶ **1 Read the text and answer the question, then complete the sentences using *go* or *come*.**

a Are the people moving towards the speaker or listener? ....

BODY LANGUAGE

'As we stand outside this building, you will notice that people are often nervous when they **(b)** .... inside to meet somebody important so they protect themselves by crossing their arms or touching some part of their clothes before they **(c)** .... inside.'

▶ **2 Complete the sentences using *come* or *go* in the correct form.**

ROYAL VISIT

A spokesman inside No 10 Downing Street, the British Prime Minister's residence, 'Every week the Prime Minister **(a)** .... to Buckingham Palace to tell the Queen about any important political problems, then he **(b)** .... back to No 10 Downing Street to tell us what the Queen said.'

G PRACTICE

▶ Think carefully about the position of the speaker and the listener before you complete these sentences with a suitable phrase including *go* or *come*.

a

There's a really interesting programme on cable television tonight about watching too much TV. As your TV is broken, why don't you _____?

b

Or, as your brother has a new colour set with stereo, we could _____.

discover, invent

12

What did Erno Rubik invent?

A DEFINITIONS

▶ **Read the definitions and decide whether scientists *invented* or *discovered*
the computer.**

discover /dɪsˈkʌvə/:   be the first person to find something that already exists, such as
a place, the truth, some information or some facts

invent /ɪnˈvent/:   be the first person to make or create something that does not
exist, such as a machine

B CONTEXT

▶ **Look at the questions and then read the text to find the answers.**

a Was the article in the Guardian newspaper true? ....

b Was the first photo in the world taken in Europe or in Asia according to the

   Guardian article? ....

c Why couldn't the public see the photo in London? ....

d According to the Guardian, the photo was first discovered and then invented in
Japan.   **True/False**

A few years ago there was a very unclear photograph of a man on the
front page of the Guardian newspaper. The article said that it was the
first picture ever taken and that it was at least seventy or more years
older than any other photo in the world. Somebody in Japan
discovered it hidden in a cave where it had been untouched for over
two centuries. Apparently an unknown Japanese scientist had
invented a special technique for making photographic negatives
before anybody in Europe.

A special exhibition was arranged just for one day for the public to
view it in London. The reason for the short viewing was because the
negative was so old and could not be left in the light for very long.
When people went there, there was nothing to see.

The article had been written on the first of April, which is April Fools'
Day, the day when people play jokes on their friends.

C PRONUNCIATION

▶ **1 Match the words with the correct stress pattern.**

a invent   i) ☐☐   ii) ☐☐

b discover   i) ☐☐☐   ii) ☐☐☐   iii) ☐☐☐

▶ **2** Does the *o* in *discover* have the same sound as the *o* in *other* or *over*?

....

D TESTING

▶ **1 Complete these sentences with *invent* or *discover* in the correct form.**

Famous Hungarians

a In 1938 the journalist, Laszlo Biro .... the ball point pen or biro.

b Szent-Gyorgyi .... the role of vitamin C.

c Professor Erno Rubik .... the rubik cube or Hungarian Horror with 43 252 003 274 489 856 000 combinations.

d The Hungarians .... the coach or *kocsi szeker*, the wagon of Kocs— the village where coaches were first made.

▶ **2 What did they say? Complete the sentences with *discover* or *invent*.**

a If God didn't exist it would be necessary to .... him.
     Voltaire (1694–1778) French writer and philosopher

b To .... something consists of seeing what everybody has seen and thinking what nobody has thought.
     Szent-Gyorgyi (1893–1986) Hungarian born US biochemist

E PRACTICE

▶ Write a sentence using the information given. Include a word from the box.

invent   discover

a ~~Easter Day 1772~~
Easter Island with its strange statues called 'moais'
Jacob Roggeveen

On Easter Day 1722, ...

b first car
Karl Benz
1885

....

bring, get, take

13

A DEFINITIONS

▶ **Read the definitions and complete the dialogues using the three verbs.**

bring /brɪŋ/:   carry or accompany to where the speaker or the listener is

take /teɪk/:   carry or accompany to a place where neither the speaker nor the listener is

get /get/:   go to a place where neither the speaker nor the listener is and return with someone or something

Charles is having a party at home. He is speaking to William on the phone.

Later William and Sarah are at home.

B PARTS OF THE VERBS

▶ **Complete the table by putting the letters in brackets in the correct order.**

infinitive	past simple	past participle
get	(gto) *got*	(tog)
take	(okto)	(ktane)
bring	(tbohrug)	(gruboth)

C CONTEXTS

▶ **Read the texts and answer the questions.**

a The last of the Yanomami of the Amazonian jungle

They take our gold and they say they bring us a better way of life. But they only bring new diseases and pollution to our territory.

Who is speaking—the gold miners or the Yonomami Indians? ....

b David's toe

An unemployed Italian walked into a Florence museum on 20 September 1991, took out a hammer, and smashed the second toe of the left foot of Michelangelo's famous marble statue of 'David'. Experts hoped to repair the damage in a few days but souvenir hunters had taken home some of the tiny pieces of the toe.

Is the writer in the same place as the pieces of David's toe? ....

c Souvenir?

Piero: What's that you've brought home?
Giorgio: Just a few bits of marble. I got them from the Galleria dell'Accademia in Florence.

i) Is Piero in the same place as the marble pieces? ....

ii) Is Giorgio in the same place as the marble pieces? ....

D CHECKING

▶ **Look at the sentences and correct any of the words in *italics* which are wrong.**

a It's too far to walk from here to the station so I'll *bring* you in my car.
b I've got to stay at home today so can you *take* these letters to the post office?
c The postman didn't *take* us any letters today.
d *Take* some money and *get* some bread. Don't worry about the rest of the shopping—your father is *bringing* it home later.
e Can you *bring* the coffee to her? She's upstairs in bed.
f Can you *bring* the coffee please? It's downstairs in the kitchen and I've got to stay up here in bed.

E TESTING

▶ **Complete the sentences using *bring, take* or *get* in the correct form.**

a My bonnie lies over the ocean, my bonnie lies over the sea.
My bonnie lies over the ocean, oh, ... back my bonnie to me.
　　Scottish song about a separated couple　　*bonnie* = darling

b You can't .... it with you when you go.
　　English proverb　　*it* = money　　*go* = die

c If a friend asks you to a Bring Your Own Bottle party, you should
.... a bottle with you, when you go. The host may ask you to
.... a special kind of drink.

d If you go to a Chinese takeaway restaurant, you can't eat the food there. You have
to .... it home. The person at your house will want you to
.... it back quickly before it gets cold. If it is really tasty, you may
decide to go out again and .... some more.

F PRACTICE

▶ **Complete the sentences with a suitable phrase. Include a different verb from the box in each sentence.**

get　bring　take

14 be dressed, dress, get dressed, have got on, put on, take off, wear

A DEFINITIONS

▶ These verbs can be put into two groups—verbs of action and verbs of state.

Action verbs

| put (clothes) on |
| get dressed /drest/ |
| dress [formal] |

| take (clothes) off |

State verbs

| have got (clothes) on |
| be dressed |
| wear /weə/ (clothes) |

▶ Which words and phrases can you use to complete these sentences? Fill in the correct numbers.

a 4. b .... c ....

a Before you have a shower, you should ...
b As soon as you get out of the shower, you should ...
c You have been getting ready for two hours. It's already 11 am, so surely you must ...

1 have got your clothes on.
2 put your clothes on.
3 be wearing your clothes.
4 take your clothes off.
5 be dressed.
6 get dressed.
7 dress.

B CONTEXT

▶ **Read the text and decide if the statement is true or false.**

The photograph shows clothes with patterns suitable for a Surma
ceremony.   **True/False**

When people get dressed for a
special ceremony, not many
would dress like the Surma in
Ethiopia. In fact, when the
Surma are dressed, they have got
very few clothes on. Rather than
spend time putting on and then
taking off a lot of clothes, the
Surma use body decoration.
First, chalk is applied and then a
painter removes it with his
fingertips to create traditional
designs. These are to frighten men or attract
women. In the distance it looks as if they are
wearing clothes with beautiful patterns on them.

C WHAT COMES AFTER THE VERBS?

▶ **Fill in the table. Decide whether the verbs can be followed by an object
and put a tick ✓ in the correct column.**

	object	no object
Example: wear	✓	
a put on		
b dress		
c get dressed		
d have got on		
e be dressed		
f take off		

NOTE: *Dress* and *be dressed* can be used with an adverb, for example, *She dresses
well*. These verbs can also be used with *in*, for example, *She always dresses in
red, I'll be dressed in a brown jacket.*

D PRONUNCIATION

a Does *wear* rhyme with *near* or *pear*? ....
b Does the last *d* in *dressed* sound like the *d* in *do* or the *t* in *to*? ....

E TESTING

▶ **1 There are mistakes in four of these sentences. Find the mistakes and correct them.**

It's late. We should get ready for the party now . . .

a Let me wear my new clothes.

b Let me dress my new clothes.

c Let me dress first.

d Let me put off my old jeans and put on something clean.

e Let me get dressed first.

f I want to be dressed first.

g Do you like what I've on?

h Do you like what I have got on?

i Do you like what I'm wearing?

j Shall I wear my new bag?

▶ **2 You can identify the nationality of Arab people from the clothes they wear. Look at the pictures and then complete the sentences. Use each of the verbs in the box once in the correct form.**

> dress   have got on   get dressed   wear
> take off   put on   be dressed

Kuwaiti   Moroccan   Sudanese   Tunisian

a How do Arab men ....?

b The Kuwaiti .... a keffiyeh.

c The Moroccan has not .... his fez .... yet.

d The Sudanese is ....

e The Tunisian .... fully .... but like all Muslims he

must .... his shoes before going into a mosque.

f Only one man .... glasses ....

52

F PRACTICE

▶ **Look at the seven situations and write a short piece of advice for each one. Use a different verb from the box in each sentence.**

~~dress~~	have got on	get dressed	wear
take off	put on	be dressed	

Example: for a job interview

.....*You should dress smartly.*.....

1 to enter a church

....

2 in cold weather

....

3 carnival in Venice

....

4 in Japan

....

5 to get married

6 in the morning

....

15 notice, realise, recognise, remark, remark on

You will see this person again, how will you recognise him?

A DEFINITIONS

▶ **Read the definitions and then answer the questions.**

notice /'nəʊtɪs/:   be aware of, see* somebody or something
realise /'rɪəlaɪz/:   know something after thinking about it
recognise /'rekəgnaɪz/:   know somebody or something, because you remember them/ it, you have seen* them/it before
remark /rɪ'mɑːk/:   say a few words about somebody or something. This word can only be used before indirect speech or after direct speech.
remark on /ri'mɑːk/:   say a few words about something
                     * or hear/d or taste/d or smell/smelt or feel/felt

a When people meet what do you think they normally notice first, the other person's

 ears, hair or eyes? ....

b Do you realise there is a mistake on a bill before you get it, before you check it or

 after you check it? ....

c Is it easier to recognise someone you knew years ago or your mother?

 ....

d Which one of the following is incorrect?
  i) He remarked on the weather.
  ii) He remarked the weather.
  iii) He remarked that the weather was hot.

B CONTEXT

► **1 Read the story and decide if this is a picture of the barman or the customer.**

In the Bar

I went slowly into the pub. I was afraid the barman would recognise me from the past. He looked at me and then he noticed the blood on my head. 'That's a bad cut,' he remarked. I was surprised he didn't remark on the way I limped in. I tried to speak but no words came. It was then that he realised that I had been shot. I knew that I was bleeding badly. He suddenly moved towards me and ...

► **2 Now answer these questions about the text.**

a Had the barman seen the customer before? ....

b What unusual thing did the barman see when he looked at the customer?

....

c What didn't the barman say anything about? ....

d When did the barman know the customer had been shot—immediately or after he had looked carefully at the customer's condition?

....

C PRONUNCIATION

▶ **Match the words with the correct stress pattern.**

a recognise   i) ☐☐☐   ii) ☐☐☐   iii) ☐☐☐

b realise   i) ☐☐☐   ii) ☐☐☐   iii) ☐☐☐

c notice   i) ☐☐   ii) ☐☐

d remark   i) ☐☐   ii) ☐☐

D WHAT COMES AFTER THE VERB?

▶ **Read the notes and then decide which words and phrases can complete the sentences.**

realise	can be followed by a clause Example: *The barman realised the customer was in trouble.*
remark	can be followed by a clause Example: *The barman remarked that the weather was hot.* can come after direct speech Example: *'You seem to be worried,' he remarked.*
remark on	something Example: *He remarked on my shaking hand.* somebody + something Example: *He remarked on the customer's hand.* but not *He remarked on the customer.*

▶ **1 Fill in the correct numbers.**

a ..1. .2. .5. b .... c .... d ....

a He noticed   1 the criminal.
b He realised   2 that I was wounded.
c He remarked   3 on the blood.
d He recognised   4 on how bad the cut was.
                  5 my gun.

▶ **2 Fill in the correct number .....**

'You are bleeding,'   1 he noticed.
                       2 he realised.
                       3 he remarked.
                       4 he remarked on.
                       5 he recognised.

E TESTING

▶ **1 Read the dialogue between the bar manager and the barman, then complete the sentences using the words in the box.**

| realise   recognise   remark   notice |

Barman in danger

Manager:

Barman:

(a) .... Did you really the stranger?

Not immediately. A little bit later I knew I had seen him before.

(b) .... Did you his injury?

Yes. I saw it immediately.

(c) .... Did you how much danger you were in?

No. I had no idea.

(d) .... Did you on the cut?

Yes. I said something about it.

▶ **2 Read the sentences and correct any of the verbs which are wrong.**

The soldiers are coming

a Do you recognise how many people will die if there is another World War?
b I did not remark the soldiers coming towards us.
c I suddenly realised that they had noticed me and that they had also recognised me.

F PRACTICE

▶ Look at the picture story and read what the man was thinking.

▶ Later the police interviewed the witness in the restaurant. Complete the
conversation using the information in the picture story. Use a different
word from the box in each line of the dialogue.

> realise   recognise   remark   notice

    Police: Had you seen the man before?

a **Witness:** ....
    Police: What first made you suspicious?

b **Witness:** ....
    Police: Did you speak to him?

c **Witness:** ....
    Police: Did you think that he was going to shoot you?

d **Witness:** ....

Revision C
— *units 11–15* —

1 come, go (unit 11)

▶ Read the text and look at the pictures. Then decide who would say sentence *a* and who would say sentence *b*.

Because of the large number of sharks around Surfers' Paradise in Queensland, Australia, both lifeguards and air patrols are used to warn the swimmers when sharks are approaching.

a The shark's coming towards the coast.
b The shark's going towards the coast.

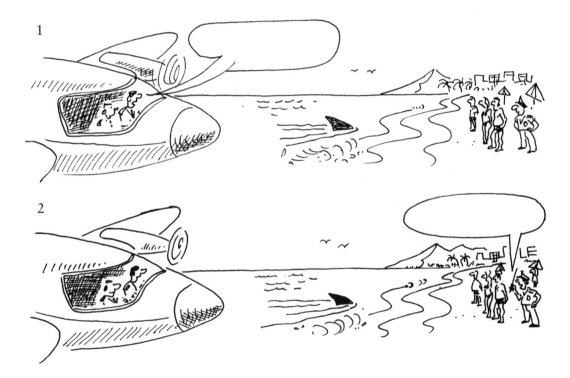

2 discover, invent (unit 12)

▶ Put the words in the right order to make a sentence which might explain some of the mysteries of the South American Indians' advanced culture.

| ~~There is a theory~~ | and then hid the plans | the aeroplane 500 years ago |

| which were never | that somebody | invented | discovered. |

There is a theory ....

3 bring, get, take (unit 13)

▶ **What are these people saying? Write a sentence using a word or phrase from each column.**

	get	the bread.
I'll	take	the chocolates.
	bring	the flowers.

4 be dressed, dress, get dressed, have got on, notice, put on, realise, recognise, remark, remark on, take off, wear (units 14–15)

▶ **Find the answers to all the questions in the box.**

wear	put on	dress
get dressed	take off	have got on
be dressed	realise	recognise
notice	remark	remark on

a Which two words are complete opposites? ....

b Which word is connected with memory? ....

c Which word suggests that after thinking carefully you know something?

   ....

d Which word is connected with speech and takes an object? ....

e Which word is used with direct speech? ....

f Which words can be used to complete these sentences?

   i) He didn't .... the broken window until he had been sitting in the room for five minutes.

   ii) .... he ....? I think that he ....

   already .... his big coat ....

   iii) Go and ....

   iv) Go and ....

   v) The bride .... a white dress and carried yellow roses.

16 check, control, examine, test

> # HOW LONG
> ## IS IT SINCE
> ### YOU HAD YOUR
> **EYES TESTED?**

A DEFINITIONS

▶ **Read the definitions and then complete the sentences.**

check /tʃek/: make sure something is all right, correct or safe
examine /ɪgˈzæmɪn/: look at in detail
test /test/: find out what people or things are like and/or how well they work
control /kənˈtrəʊl/: have direct influence or power over a system or situation

a A security guard may .... or .... your bag as you go into a building.

b The only way to see if a radio is really working is to .... it.

c Governments always want to try to .... inflation.

B CONTEXTS

▶ **1 Read the three texts quickly and decide which is about being healthy naturally.** ....

▶ **2 Decide if the statement which follows each text is true or false.**

a Most misspelt name

Almost every time that Edward Nedelcov of Regina, Canada, checks how his surname has been spelt, he finds another mistake. In fact, he has found over 1000 different spellings since 1960. Among the common mistakes are Nevelcove, Neddlecough, Middlecou, and Needochou. His favourite spelling is on a letter from the Queen of England. It is addressed to E.A. Dedelcov.

The Queen's secretary had checked the spelling of Edward's name. **True/False**

b Quite a shock

The most powerful nuclear bomb ever was tested on 30 October 1961 in the USSR. The shock wave circled the world three times, taking over 36 hours for the first circuit.

The scientists wanted to see if the bomb would work properly.   **True/False**

c Ayurveda

According to the ancient Indian system of healthcare known as 'Ayurveda', the body is controlled by three principles called 'doshas'.

Vata dosha controls movement.
Pitta dosha controls metabolism, the way the body uses food.
Kapha dosha controls structure, for example, the size of your body and bones.

If one dosha is out of balance, it can cause illness. For example, if Vata is out of balance, the person becomes worried and the blood pressure may go up. The way to perfect health, says Ayurveda, is to keep the three doshas in balance.

When an Ayurvedic doctor examines you, he takes great care to find out which dosha is strongest in you. Then he will recommend the right kind of diet and exercise, herbs and meditation to balance that dosha.

 i) Vata dosha controls the circulation of the blood.   **True/False**
ii) An Ayurvedic doctor examines you to discover imbalances in the
    body.   **True/False**

C PRONUNCIATION

▶ **1 Match the words with the correct stress pattern.**

a control   i) ☐⬜   ii) ⬜☐

b examine   i) ⬜☐☐   ii) ☐⬜☐   iii) ☐☐⬜

▶ **2** Does *examine* rhyme with *wine* or *win*? ....

D CHECKING

▶ **Look at the text and correct any of the words in *italics* which are wrong.**

1 When you enter a foreign country, immigration officers *control* your passport to see
   that it is valid. If they think something is wrong, they will *examine* the signature,
   the photograph, all the visas, and the pages. If they are quite sure that there is a
   problem, they can arrange to have the passport *tested* scientifically to see if it is
5 genuine or a forgery. One of the ways to *test* the movement of people in and out of
   a country is by this regular *checking*.

E PRACTICE

▶ **Read the text and then complete the sentences with a suitable word or phrase. Include a different verb from the box in each sentence.**

> check   test   control   examine

Perfect sight without glasses

An American called Bates wrote a book explaining simple eye exercises which can improve eyesight and even help people to give up wearing glasses. With regular practice at home amazing results are possible. Aldous Huxley, the author, was nearly blind when he started similar exercises and his sight returned to normal.

Some say that opticians are not in favour of these techniques because they don't want to lose their position in the profitable eyesight business.

Of course, it is a good idea to visit an optician from time to time. A good optician will not only ask you to read words and letters from a distance, but he will also take a careful look into your eyes. This will take about half an hour.

How good are your eyes? If you cannot read this from a distance of two metres, you would be well advised to take up Bates's exercises.

a If you practise Bates's exercises regularly, you can ....

b A good optician will spend 30 minutes ....

c If you are not happy with your eyesight, get a copy of Bates's book and ....

....

d Trying to read this from two metres is an easy way to ....

game, match, play

What game is it?

A DEFINITIONS

▶ **Read the information then decide whether sentence *a* or *b* is about sport.**

a It was great play.
b It was a great play.

game /geɪm/:	i) general meaning—a sport or pastime with rules and someone tries to win
	ii) specific meaning—a match
match /mætʃ/:	an organised game of football, chess or other sport or pastime, a contest
play /pleɪ/:	i) style or standard of action such as *fair play*, *exciting play*, *bad play*
	ii) action in a contest, for example: *Rain stopped play.*
	iii) take part in a game (verb).

WARNING: The noun *play* with the article *a* has no connection with sport. So the sentence *I saw a play* is only about drama in a theatre, such as Shakespeare's 'Hamlet' and **never** about sport.

B CONTEXT

▶ **Read the text and find out the name of the sport, then see if the description matches the picture.**

Name the game

It is a three-a-side game on a large court, with fast play. The ball is made of rattan (a cane material) and you cannot touch it with hands or arms. So it is something like volleyball with your hands tied behind your back. It is probably of Indian origin but it is now played so much in South East Asia that it is part of the Asian Games. Matches at international level are becoming more and more frequent. The game is, of course, Sepak Takrow.

C PRONUNCIATION

Does the *a* in *match* have the same sound as the *ar* in *arch*, the *u* in *cut* or the *a* in *cat*? ....

D WHAT COMES AFTER THE WORD?

GENERAL RULES

game	of	sport Example: *a game of basketball, a game of hockey**
match		comes immediately after the sport Example: *a basketball match, a hockey match*
play		does not have an article (*a* or *the*) when talking about sport Example: *Nice play!, Play will start soon.*

*In American English *game* means *match*, and so comes after the sport, for example, *a basketball game.*

E CHECKING

▶ **Read the text and correct any of the words in *italics* which are wrong.**

1 Anyone for a *match* of korfball?

Korfball is not everybody's favourite *play*. In fact many people have never seen the *match* played. It is similar to basketball but it is always played with six men and six women in each team. The name of the *game* comes from the Dutch word 'korfbal',
5 which means basketball. Like basketball, it has a lot of fast *play* especially in international *matches*.

F TESTING

▶ **Which text is about**

1 a game? ....

2 a match? ....

3 play? ....

a The Cameroons beat Argentina in the first round of the 1990 World Cup in Italy.

b In the last five minutes Lineker kicked the ball beautifully into the back of the goal.

c My favourite is *shogi*. It is a type of Japanese chess.

G PRACTICE

▶ **Complete these questions about sport with a suitable phrase. Include a different noun from the box in each sentence.**

| play   game   match |

a Did .... ?
Yes. I saw it live. Real Madrid 6–Milano 6.

b Have .... ?
No. But I know the rules. You play it in a room with a racket and a little ball. It is a bit like tennis but you use the wall instead of a net.

c Wasn't .... ?
Yes, that was the most exciting five minutes I've ever seen in baseball and there is still another thirty minutes left.

18 excursion, journey, travel, trip, voyage

How far can a snail travel in $2\frac{1}{2}$ minutes?

A WHAT ARE THE DIFFERENCES?

▶ Look at the questions and then read the explanations to find the answers.

a Decide which words can be used to talk about going from one place to another by land. _Travel, journey, trip, excursion_

b Which of the nouns is uncountable? _travel_

travel /ˈtrævəl/: abstract noun	the general idea of going from place to place
travel verb	go from place to place
voyage /ˈvɔɪdʒ/or /vɔɪdʒ/: noun	long distance travel, by sea or in space, often for exploration; you do not have to return
journey /ˈdʒɜːnɪ/: noun	movement between two places, either on one particular occasion for long distances or on a regular basis, for example, going to work, usually by land
trip /trɪp/: noun	a visit somewhere for pleasure or business, often for a short time; you have to return
excursion /ɪkˈskɜːʃən/: noun	a short visit somewhere for pleasure or a particular purpose for a few hours; you usually go by train, coach or pleasure boat as part of a group and return the same day

B CONTEXTS

▶ Read the texts and decide which talks about the longest distance and which the shortest distance.

The longest journey is ....

The shortest journey is...

a Going on unknown voyages

Voyager Two is making man's greatest voyage. It travels at 1 666 666 kilometres per hour and has already left our solar system. Nobody knows when earth will lose contact with this spaceship.

Until the 16th century it was believed that the earth was flat and sailors going on long voyages would live in fear of falling over the edge of the world.

b To travel or not to travel?
Travel is the best education a person can have. It opens our eyes to other cultures, languages, religions and races.

c How slow is fast?
The fastest snail on record travelled 33cm in 2 min 31 sec in England in 1988.

d The most travelled man?
Jesse Hart Rosdail (1914–77) from Elmshurst, Illinois, USA, visited more countries than anyone else. He went on both long and short trips by train, plane and ship visiting 215 countries and territories and never staying anywhere long. North Korea and French Antarctic Territories were the only countries he never went to. Very few foreigners can make a trip to North Korea.

e Crossing the wall
Not long ago many people died when they tried to cross the Berlin Wall from East to West Berlin. In 1989 when the Wall was opened, groups would go on day excursions to shop. Now that the Wall has gone these excursions are a thing of the past.

f Great journeys
Nick Danziger went on a journey across Europe to China. He went by bicycle and without permission. Another traveller made a journey by foot across Africa from Cape Town to Cairo. Last century someone rode a horse from the top of North America to the bottom of South America.

C CHECKING   *TRAVEL types*

▶ **Complete the table by putting a tick ✓ in the right columns.**

	long short distance		only short time at destination	pleasure	serious	land	sea/ air/ space
Example: journey	✓	✓		✓	✓	✓	✓
a voyage							
b trip							
c excursion							
d travel							

D PRONUNCIATION

▶ **1** *Voyage* can be pronounced with one or two syllables; when it is pronounced with two syllables, does the last syllable have the same sound as *age*, *large*, or *fridge*? ....

► **2 Match the words with the correct stress pattern.**

a voyage   i) □▢   ii) ☑□

b journey   i) □▢   ii) ☑□

c travel   i) □▢   ii) ☑□

d excursion   i) □□▢   ii) □☑□   iii) ▢□□

E WHAT CAN GO WITH THE WORD?

► **Decide if the following table and information is correct.**

a	go on/make	a trip a voyage a journey	Correct/Incorrect
b	go on	an excursion	Correct/Incorrect
c	do	a trip a voyage a journey an excursion	Correct/Incorrect
d	do/make/go on	a travel	Correct/Incorrect

travel (v.)

F TESTING

► **Fill the gaps with the correct words and phrases from the box. Some words may be used more than once.**

> space   business   half day   different types of
> down the river   across the Kalahari desert
> along the old Silk Road from China to Europe
> sightseeing   to the South Seas   to the stars

Example: a A travel _business_
             b _Space_ .... travel
             c _Different types of_ travel

1 a A voyage _down the river_
   b A voyage _to the South Seas_
   c A voyage _to the stars_

2 a A journey ....
   b A journey ....
   c A journey ....
   d A journey ....
   e A journey ....

3 a An excursion _across the Kalahari desert_
   b A _space_ excursion
   c A .... excursion

4 a A trip ....
   b A trip ....
   c A trip ....
   d A trip ....
   e A trip ....
   f A _half day_ trip
   g A _sightseeing_ trip
   h A .... trip

G PRACTICE

► Write one sentence for each situation. Include a different noun from the box in each sentence.

| travel   voyage   trip   excursion   journey |

1

In 1770, Captain Cook *made a voyage to Australia*

2

CAMBRIDGE
SATURDAY

Leave 8.00
Return 22.00
Cost £16
Tickets — Reception

3

Database Products
MEMO
TO: *Selina Roach*
FROM: *William Shaw*
DATE: *Tuesday*
Selina, Had to go to Tokyo.
Meeting postponed.
Back in a week.   William.

There is *an excursion to Cambridge on Saturday*

William Shaw *has gone on a business trip to Tokyo*

4

5

Travel is
the best
way to
learn about
life.

How long *is the journey from London to Paris* ?

71

19 excuse me, here you are, pardon, please, sorry, there you are

A WHAT ARE THE DIFFERENCES?

▶ Read the explanations and then answer the questions below.

please /pliːz/: i) used at the start or end of the sentence for polite requests; used in the middle with heavy stress if the speaker is annoyed
ii) used to accept offers—'Yes, please.'
not used to ask people to repeat something
not used when giving people things

here/there you are: used when passing or giving things to people

excuse me /ɪkˈskjuz/: i) used before doing or saying something which might annoy, disturb or interrupt somebody
ii) used to get somebody's attention
iii) used after you sneeze or cough
not used to ask people to repeat (except in US English) **nor** used to apologise

sorry /ˈsɒrɪ/: i) *sorry* used with falling intonation to apologise after doing or saying something which might be a problem for somebody

ii) *sorry* used with rising intonation if we do not hear somebody to ask them to repeat
not used to get someone's attention

pardon /ˈpɑːdn/: *pardon* used with rising intonation if we do not hear somebody to ask them to repeat

What do you say a if someone says something very unclearly? ....
b if you ask someone to sit down? ....
c if you step on someone's foot?...
d if you want to get off the bus and people are standing in the way? ....
e if you pass someone their umbrella?...
f if someone offers you a cup of tea? ....

B CONTEXTS

▶ **Look at each question and then read the text to find the answer.**

a Are Angela's requests successful? ....

Turn it down

Angela: Peter! Could you turn the TV down please?
[There is no response]
[louder now] Peter! Could you turn the TV down, please?
Peter: [Shouts] Pardon? Sorry? I can't hear you.
Angela: [even louder] Could you **please** turn down the television?
[volume of TV is reduced] **Thank you!**
Peter: There's no need to shout.
Angela: I'm sorry!
Peter: That's all right.

b Are all the customer's requests successful? ....

No food?

Customer: Excuse me!
Waiter: Yes, sir?
Customer: Please could we see the menu?
Waiter: Yes, of course, sir. Sorry. Here you are.
Customer: Thank you. Erm, I think we'll have the fish, please.
Waiter: The fish?
Customer: Yes, please.
Waiter: I'm sorry, sir, there's no fish today.
Customer: Very well, the steak.
Waiter: I'm really sorry, sir, there's no steak left.
Customer: What! No fish, no steak! Very well, could I see the manager, please?
Waiter: I'm extremely sorry, sir, it's his day off.

c Both dialogues contain polite requests and apologies. **True/False**

C PRONUNCIATION

▶ **1 Which syllable has the stress in**

a pardon? ....
b excuse me? ....
c sorry? ....

▶ **2 Which two syllables have stress in *Here you are*? ....**

▶ **3 *Pardon* rhymes with *garden*. True/False**

▶ **4 a Which is an apology and which is a request to repeat?**
i) *Sorry?* ....   ii) *Sorry!* ....
b Does the voice rise in the question or the exclamation? ....

D CHECKING

▶ **Look at the conversation and change any of the words in *italics* which are incorrect.**

1 **Mike:** *Pardon*. I didn't mean to push you.
  Sarah: That's all right.
  Mike: Is this seat free?
  Sarah: Yes. *Excuse me* do sit down.
5 **Mike:** Would you like some tea?
  Sarah: *Yes, please.*
  Mike: *Excuse me,* could you pass the sugar?
  Sarah: *Sorry?*
  Mike: I asked if you could pass the sugar.
10 **Sarah:** *Please.*
  Mike: Thank you.

  Mike: Atchoo! *Pardon!* (Mike goes to the bathroom)

  Sam: *Pardon,* could I sit here?
  Sarah: *Sorry,* it's somebody's seat.

E PRACTICE

▶ **Complete the dialogues using all the expressions in the box.**

excuse me   pardon   sorry!   sorry?   here you are   please

Example: **A:** ..... *Sorry?* .....
              B: I said, have you got the right time, please?

1 **A:** (steps on B's toe) .....
  B: That's all right.
2 **A:** Could you pass the sugar, please?

  B: .....
3 **A:** Can you hear me?

  B: .....
  A: CAN YOU HEAR ME?
4 **A:** Would you like some more coffee?

  B: Yes, ...

5 **A:** .....
  B: What a terrible cough you've got!

bored, boring, excited, exciting, interested, interesting

What is so exciting about javelin throwing?

A DEFINITIONS

▶ **Read the definitions and answer the questions with one of the words below.**

interesting /ˈɪntrəstɪŋ/: causing interest
interested /ˈɪntrəstɪd/: showing interest
exciting /ɪkˈsaɪtɪŋ/: causing excitement
excited /ɪkˈsaɪtɪd/: showing excitement
boring /ˈbɔːrɪŋ/: causing boredom
bored /bɔːd/: showing boredom

1 How would you describe   **a** a good detective film? ....

   b a documentary film on a scientific subject you know

   a lot about? ....

   c how you feel during a long, bad speech?

   ....

   d how you feel about good news about a wonderful

   new job? ....

   e how you feel during a TV programme on a hobby of

   yours? ....

   f a long, bad speech? ....

2 **a** Which is the action?   *-ing* or *-ed*
   b Which is the reaction?   *-ing* or *-ed*
   c Which is active?   *-ing* or *-ed*
   d Which is passive?   *-ing* or *-ed*

B CONTEXT

▶ **Read the conversation about athletics and decide if the statements are true or false.**

a Bob and Tom are interested in the same athletics events.   **True/False**
b Bob finds short distance races boring.   **True/False**
c Tom isn't interested in sprinting.   **True/False**
d Bob was really excited by the 100 metres final on TV.   **True/False**
e Bob doesn't find javelin throwing exciting.   **True/False**
f Tom gets bored with the marathon. **True/False**

Bob: Listen, this is really interesting—in the 1988 Olympic Games, Ben Johnson and Carl Lewis *both* reached a speed of 43.37 kph in the 100 metres final!
Tom: Sorry, I'm not really interested in track events such as 100 and 400 metres.
Bob: I actually saw the race on TV—it was really exciting.
Tom: I was far more excited by the javelin final—Petra Felke throwing a record 74.68 metres.
Bob: How can you call the javelin event exciting? All that waiting between throws.
Tom: The most boring event has got to be the marathon—almost two hours watching runner after runner go past.
Bob: You wouldn't be bored if you were *in* the race!

C PRONUNCIATION

▶ **1   How many syllables are there in**

a interested? ....
b bored? ....
c interesting? ....

▶ **2   Where is the stress in**

a interesting? ....
b excited? ....

D WHAT COMES BEFORE AND AFTER THE WORDS?

GENERAL RULES

be	interested in excited about/by bored with/by	someone something	find	someone something	interesting exciting boring

E CHECKING

▶ Read the sentences and correct the words in *italics* if they are wrong.

a I'm very *interesting in* photography.
b I didn't enjoy the film because I was *boring*.
c I would be very *interested of* going to see that play.
d I am very *excited from* my new camera.

F TESTING

▶ Match the sentences on the left with the responses on the right.

1 You were very boring at the party.
2 You were very bored at the party.
3 You were very interesting at the party.
4 You were very interested at the party.
5 You were very excited at the party.
6 You were very exciting at the party.

a Yes, everyone seemed to be listening to me.
b Yes, everyone was falling asleep.
c Yes, it was a great conversation.
d Yes, I don't like playing games.
e Yes, people started to shout and scream when I did an imitation of a ghost.
f Yes, I know, I was jumping up and down like a child.

G PRACTICE

▶ Here is an interview with British athlete, John Regis, who runs in 100 and 200 metre races. Complete the reporter's questions and use one word from each pair in the box.

bored	—boring
excited	—exciting
interested	—interesting

a Reporter: What part of the race .... ?

   John: Waiting for it to begin—it seems to last forever!

b Reporter: When .... ?

   John: Oh, when you are about ten metres from the finishing line and you're not sure who is going to win but you think <u>you</u> are!

c Reporter: Which .... ?

   John: Planning out my exact training programme after one season has finished in preparation for the next season. Because this takes a lot of careful thought.

Revision D
units 16–20

1 check, control, examine, test (unit 16)

▶ Look at the speech bubbles and correct any of the words in *italics* which are wrong.

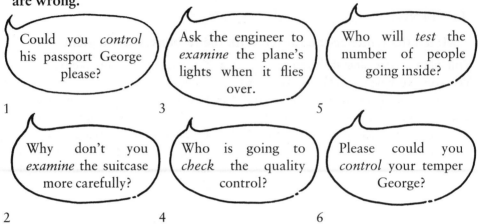

Could you *control* his passport George please?

1

Ask the engineer to *examine* the plane's lights when it flies over.

3

Who will *test* the number of people going inside?

5

Why don't you *examine* the suitcase more carefully?

2

Who is going to *check* the quality control?

4

Please could you *control* your temper George?

6

2 game, match, play (unit 17)

▶ Complete the sentences with a phrase from Box A and a phrase from Box B. Put the numbers of the answers in the box and add up the numbers to check that your answers are correct.

	A	B	
1	7	10	= 18
2			= 16
3			= 22
4			= 22

1 It was a great game, ...
2 It was a great match, ...
3 It was great play, ...
4 It was a great play, ...

A
5 Harlem Globetrotters 101 Moscow Dynamos 100—
6 by Shakespeare,
7 the Aztecs called it 'Ball Court',
8 it all happened in the first few minutes, they kept passing the ball so quickly. The crowd went crazy,

B | 9 | people in seventy-five countries watched it.
10 | but now the rules have changed and it is called basketball.
11 | but it was all over in a couple of minutes.
12 | which was so popular that it ran every night for six years.

3 excursion, journey, travel, trip, voyage (unit 18)

▶ Match words, definitions, and examples in five sets of one rectangle, one circle and one triangle.

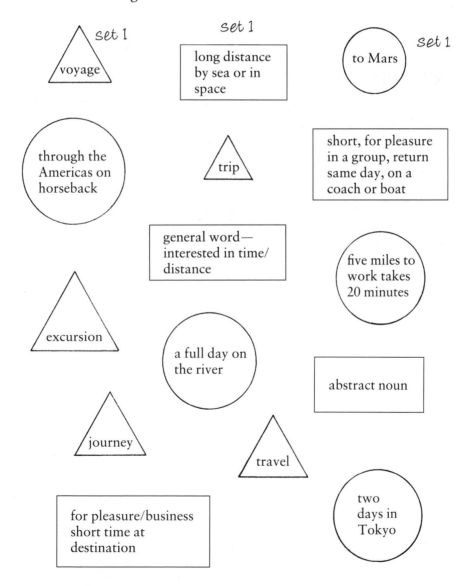

4 excuse me, here you are, pardon, please, sorry, there you are (unit 19)

▶ Put the dialogue about a misunderstanding between a waiter and a customer in a restaurant in the right order.

a One coffee!
b Could I have the bill, please?
c Sorry!
d Excuse me, I only had one.
e There you are, sir.
f The bill, please.
g Sorry? One what?
h Pardon?

5 *-ed, -ing* (unit 20)

▶ Find two logical sentences from the words below. To complete them you must decide if the circles contain *-ing* or *-ed*.

a

It is easier	interog◯ in filmstars	because I

b

I am more	to be interest◯ in politics	than to

find	interest◯	in politicians.
be	them	more excit◯ .

alive, life, live, lively

21

A WHAT ARE THE DIFFERENCES?

life /laɪf/:   noun

                    NOTE: the plural is *lives* /laɪvz/

live /lɪv/:   verb

live /laɪv/:   adjective to describe **things** or **animals**

alive /əˈlaɪv/:   adjective used to describe **people** or **animals**—it cannot be used before a noun

lively /ˈlaɪvlɪ/:   adjective which means full of human/animal energy

▶ **Which of the three adjectives above would you use to best describe**

1   2   3

....

B CONTEXTS

▶ **Match the five sentences with the person who would probably say or write them.**

a depressed person   a man in love   a radio announcer

the sheriff in an American Western   an old and experienced person

a Live for today, plan for tomorrow, learn from yesterday.

b Life has no meaning.

c

d The live broadcast will be heard by people in every continent.

e Oh! She has such a lively personality and her eyes seem to dance when she talks.

C PRONUNCIATION

▶ **Which of the following words have the same sound as the *i* in *with* and which have the same sound as the *i* in *side*? Put a tick ✓ in the correct column.**

	with	side
Example: a live show		✓
a our lives		
b She lives here.		
c life		
d alive		
e lively		
f to live		

D CHECKING

▶ **1 Read the sentences and correct any of the words in *italics* which are wrong.**

a My *alive* grandmother, goes swimming and horse riding every day.
b My grandmother, who is still *live*, *lives* a very *lively life*.
c Is there any difference between *live* and death?
d In *life* we have to *live* our *lives* as best we can. In death we do not know if we are *live* or dead.

▶ **2 What is the difference in meaning in each of the following pairs of sentences?**

a i) My grandmother is going to be on a *live* TV show.
  ii) My grandmother is going to be on a *lively* TV show.

....

b i) They were still *alive* in the house when I arrived.
  ii) They were still *living* in the house when I arrived.

....

E TESTING

▶ **Complete these sentences with a suitable word from the box.**

live (verb) live (adjective) alive life lively

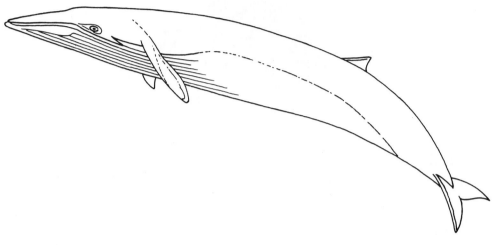

a How much longer can the minke whale ....?
b This time next year, will the minke whale still be ....?
c The minke whale is in danger. How can we save its ....?
d Most people feel sick and helpless, if they watch the killing of a minke whale on TV when the programme is ....
e These lovely animals can play in the sea for hours. They are so ....

F PRACTICE

▶ **Complete these questions about the minke whale with a suitable phrase. Include a different verb from the box in each sentence.**

live (verb) live (adjective) alive life lively

a Is ....?
Yes, quite long. It is about thirty or forty years for a healthy whale.

b How long ....?
Only a few more years unless the killing stops.

c Are ....?
Yes. Very. They jump out of the water and play for hours.

d Is ....?
Yes. I have just switched the TV on and it is coming direct from NHK the Japanese TV station.

e Is ....?
No. It has just died.

22 dead, death, die, died

When did the dodo die?

A CONTEXTS

▶ **Read the texts and answer the questions.**

a Do the sentence and the writing on the gravestone express a similar idea?

....

Death is just a long sleep.

b How many verbs are there in this slogan? ....

Don't DRINK and D R I V E

c Why was the action of the insurance company illegal?

....

He didn't drink, he never visited friends, he never travelled, he never loved.
When he died, the insurance company refused to pay his life insurance
policy because, as he never lived, he never died.

B PRONUNCIATION

a Does *dead* rhyme with *head* or *need*? ....
b Does *death* rhyme with *teeth* or *breath*? ....

C WHAT ARE THE DIFFERENCES?

GENERAL RULES

dead	adjective
die	regular verb (die, died, died) It cannot be followed by an object, so it has no passive form.
death	noun

▶ Only two of the infinitives in the box are correct. Which one describes

a a state? ....

b a change? ....

> to die   to die somebody   to be died   to be dead
> to dead   to died   to be die

D CHECKING

▶ **Match these sets of opposites.**

dead   life
die   lived
death   alive
died   live

E TESTING

▶ **1 There are mistakes in some of these sentences about the dinosaur (an animal which lived during the Ice Age). Find the mistakes and correct them.**

a When did the dinosaur dead?
b When was the death of the dinosaur?
c The dinosaur has been die for 70 million years.
d The dinosaur has already die.
e The dinosaur is dead.
f Why did the dinosaur die?
g The dinosaur was died 70 million years ago.
h How long has the dinosaur been dead?

▶ **2 Put the words in the mixed-up sentences in the correct order and include one of the missing words in the box in each sentence.**

die   die   dead   death

a There is no pain like /../the/friend./a/of

b It is better to .... on/feet/your/to/live/than/on your knees.
Dolores Ibarruri—La Pasionaria (1895–1988) Spanish politician and great believer in fighting for personal freedom.

c Only ..../swim/fish/with the tide.

d I hate your ideas but I am ready to ..../right/your/for/to express them.
Voltaire (1694–1778) French writer and philosopher

F PRACTICE

▶ **Read the text and then complete the questions about the dodo, including a word from the box.**

The dodo (the pronunciation rhymes with so-so) was a large bird that could not fly. It had short thick legs and grey feathers. It lived on the island of Mauritius near the east coast of Africa. The last dodo was killed over 300 years ago. The name dodo comes from the Portuguese word 'doido' which means stupid or crazy. In English there is an expression 'as dead as a dodo' which is used for something or somebody that is 100% dead.

die   dead   death

a How long ....?

b When ....?

c Was ....?

another, other

23

ဒါဟာ ၁ က၁ က၁သ၁စက၁း ဆိုတ၁သ၆သိ ပါသလ၁း ။

This is the Burmese alphabet. How many other alphabets are there in South East Asia?

A DEFINITIONS

▶ Read the four definitions, then put a tick ✓ in the correct columns in the table.

another /ə'nʌðə/:   means one more
the other /'ʌðə/:   means the second when there are only two
the others /'ʌðəz/:   means the rest in a group
others /'ʌðəz/:   means some of the rest in a group

	singular	plural	definite	indefinite
Example: another	✓			✓
a others				
b the other				
c the others				

B CONTEXT

▶ Look at the alphabets and then read the information on the next page and then decide if the statements which follow are true or false.

Africa
Amharic:
(from Ethiopia)

ልሆኑን: ፆንፆ ' ያወጭካን ?

Asia
Korean: 이것이 어느 나라 말인지 아시겠읍니까?
Japanese: これが 何語か わかりますか。

Europe
Modern Greek: Γνωρίζετε ποιά γλώσσα είναι αυτή ;
Russian: Вы знаете , на каком это языке?

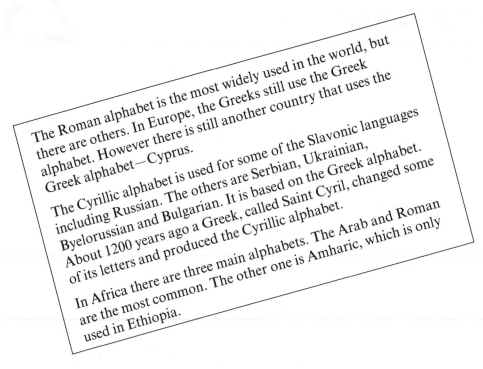

The Roman alphabet is the most widely used in the world, but there are others. In Europe, the Greeks still use the Greek alphabet. However there is still another country that uses the Greek alphabet—Cyprus.

The Cyrillic alphabet is used for some of the Slavonic languages including Russian. The others are Serbian, Ukrainian, Byelorussian and Bulgarian. It is based on the Greek alphabet. About 1200 years ago a Greek, called Saint Cyril, changed some of its letters and produced the Cyrillic alphabet.

In Africa there are three main alphabets. The Arab and Roman are the most common. The other one is Amharic, which is only used in Ethiopia.

a The other country, besides Greece, that uses the Greek alphabet is Ethiopia.   **True/False**

b Apart from Ethiopia there are other countries that use Amharic.   **True/False**

c Bulgarian is written using another alphabet apart from Cyrillic.   **True/False**

d The other alphabets shown which are not described in the text are Korean, Burmese and Japanese.   **True/False**

C WHAT CAN GO WITH THE WORD?

▶ 1 The word *other* can be combined with the articles *the* and *an.*

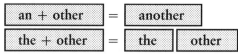

▶ Are these sentences true or false?

a *Another* is made from the two words *an + other* but is always written as one word.   **True/False**

b *The another* is a mistake.   **True/False**

▶ **2 It is not necessary to use a noun after *another* and *other*, if you have already mentioned the noun before. There are always three possible combinations.**

Example:

Give me another idea.	Give me the other idea.
or Give me another one.	or Give me the other one.
or Give me another.	or Give me the other.
Give me other ideas.	Give me the other ideas.
or Give me other ones.	or Give me the other ones.
or Give me others.	or Give me the others.

▶ **Now write all the combinations for**

a Show him another coat. ....

b Let her see the other dresses. ....

c Have you got any other hats? ....

d I prefer the other suit. ....

D CHECKING

▶ **Only one of these five paragraphs uses the words *other* and *another* correctly. Try to find it and then correct the mistakes in the other four.**

a This recipe for Chinese eight jewel duck is too complicated. Can you give me *other* one?

b I have several. Look at this one and if you don't like it I can show you *the other*.

c The problem is you have to take the skin off the bone. Some people find it easy, *another* find it too difficult.

d The Chinese do not waste any part of the duck. There are two ways of using up the parts you do not roast. Firstly you can make a soup with the bones. *Other* way is to use the fat on the skin instead of oil.

e I have some of the ingredients but where can I buy *the others*, such as water chestnuts and Chinese mushrooms?

E PRONUNCIATION

▶ **1 Is the *o* in *other* like the *o* in *son* or in *not*?** ....

▶ **2 Match the following with the correct stress pattern.**

a other   i) □▢   ii) ▢□

b another   i) □▢□   ii) □□▢   iii) ▢□□

c the other   i) □▢□   ii) □□▢   iii) ▢□□

F TESTING

▶ **Complete the puzzle using the words in the box.**

the others   others   another   other   the other

There are six boys in one family. Three of the boys have one mother, but (a) .... brothers have (b) .... mothers. Does that mean there are three step-mothers or is there (c) ...., and has the father had two wives or are there (d) ....? Now he loves his present wife but he does not love (e) ....

G PRACTICE

▶ **Complete these sentences with a suitable word or phrase. Include a different word(s) from the box in each sentence.**

another   others   the other   the others

a I have two brothers. I love one but ....

b I have finished my beer, barman, can you .... ?

c I have a contract to clean the windows in the Empire State Building. I've finished two floors and now I have ....

d Some people like raw fish but ....

ท่านรู้ไหมว่านี่คือภาษาอะไร ?

Here is Thai, another of the seven alphabets in South East Asia.

during, for, since, while

24

Modern Man has been on our planet for only four hours.

A WHAT ARE THE DIFFERENCES?

▶ **Read the explanations, then complete the sentences on the next page with words from the box.**

for /fə/:	is used before **periods** of time.
	Example: *I watched TV for two hours yesterday.*
since /sɪns/:	is used with **points** of time.
	Example: *I have been watching TV since 1 o'clock.*
during /djʊərɪŋ/:	is used to say that something happens **inside** a particular period of time. It is often used before 'determiners', which are words such as *a, the*; *my, his*; *some of, most of*; *that, these* and a noun.
	Example: *I watched a lot of TV during the weekend. It's often cold during February.*
	WARNING: You cannot use *during* with *a* + a 'time period' alone, for example, *during a month, during a few months* and *during a year* are wrong, but *during a week of storms* or *during a stormy week* are correct.
while /waɪl/:	is used to **connect two actions** happening at the same time. It is usually followed by
	a the *-ing* form of the verb
	Example: *I fell asleep while watching TV.*
	b a clause (subject + verb)
	Example: *I fell asleep while I was watching TV.*

WARNING: You cannot use *during* instead of *while*, so *I fell asleep during watching TV* is wrong.

▶ **Complete the sentences with words from the box.**

Monday   that moment   24 hours   most of the year   six days
a long time   3 pm   last year   he was outside   ages
February   a fortnight   then   watching TV   the storm
the others were sleeping   those nine months   yesterday

a We've done nothing since

b We've done nothing for
We did nothing for

c We did nothing during

d We were doing nothing while
We did nothing while

B CONTEXT

▶ **Look at the questions and then read the text to find the answers.**

a What happened when Planet Earth was a 'child'? ....

b When did Man start growing his own food? ....

c When did Man start to destroy Planet Earth? ....

Planet Earth is 4 600 million years old. If we reduce this incredibly long period of time to an understandable concept, we can compare Earth to a person of 46 years of age. We know nothing about this person's life during the first seven years. While this person was growing up very little information was left for us. All we do know is that the Earth began to 'flower' at the age of 42. Dinosaurs did not appear until one year ago, when the planet was 45.

Mammals arrived only eight months ago; in the middle of last week human-like apes evolved into ape-like humans, and at the weekend, the last ice age covered the Earth. Modern Man has been here for four hours. During the last hour, Man has discovered agriculture. The industrial revolution began a minute ago. During those sixty seconds Modern Man has made a mess of Paradise. Since the beginning of the last minute, he has increased his numbers to enormous proportions, caused the extinction of 500 animal species, polluted the planet by burning fuels and he now stands like a naughty child, proud of what he has done. He is now on the edge of a war that will end all wars and will destroy this oasis of life in the solar system.

C PRONUNCIATION

a Does the *i* in *since* have the same sound as the *i* in *sign* or in *sing*? ....

b Does the *i* in *while* have the same sound as the *i* in *mile* or the *ea* in *meal*? ....

c Match the word with the correct stress pattern.

during   i) □▢   ii) ▢□

D CHECKING

▶ **This information is about a chimpanzee that jumped onto a Danish ship in an African port, and got a free ride to Hamburg. Correct any of the words in *italics* if they are wrong.**

a The chimp was on the ship *during* a few weeks.

b The chimp was on the top of the mast *during* the whole voyage from Africa to Europe.

c The chimp drank whisky *during* it was on the ship.

d The chimp stayed up the mast *since* the whole trip.

e The chimp would not come down *while* the police were there.

f 'The chimp has been on the ship *for* the two weeks *since* it left Africa last month,' said the captain.

g The chimp lived well *during* those two weeks.

E TESTING

▶ **Use the words in the circle to make four sentences. Include a different word from the box in each of the sentences.**

for   since   while   during

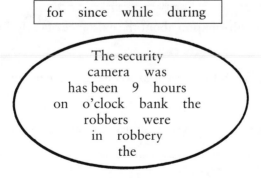

The security
camera   was
has been   9   hours
on   o'clock   bank   the
robbers   were
in   robbery
the

a ....

b ....

c ....

d ....

F PRACTICE

▶ **Read the text and then rewrite the four statements which follow so that they are correct. Include a different word from the box in each sentence.**

for since while during

The Chinese language is one of the oldest in the world. Its earliest written records go back 3000 years or more. This century some bones with Chinese characters were found dating from the ancient Shang Dynasty (1766–1123 BC). Chinese historians believe that the Chinese written language was first invented during the reign of the Yellow Emperor around 2700 BC (circa 5000 years ago).

The total number of Chinese characters is estimated at more than 50 000 of which only 5000–8000 are in common use. To help young children read these characters there is also a Chinese alphabet called 'pinyin' which they use until they have learnt the more complicated characters.

The Chinese leader Mao Tse-Tung introduced many changes to simplify the more complicated characters but some criticise this decision because young people today cannot read old texts.

a Chinese is a very modern language.

....

b Historians have no information about the existence of early Chinese characters.

....

c When young Chinese children learn to write they have no alphabet to help them.

....

d In Mao Tse-Tung's time Chinese remained the same.

....

actual, current, present

25

The actual name on my birth certificate is
'Antonio Manuel Sanpaio Soares Bentes De Oliveira'
but you can call me Tony.

A WHAT ARE THE DIFFERENCES?

▶ **Read the information and then answer the question.**

current /ˈkʌrənt/: adjective meaning existing, which suggests a limited period of time and change is expected

present /ˈprɛzənt/: adjective meaning existing, which suggests an open period of time and change is not expected

actual /ˈæktʃʊəl/: adjective meaning real
Example: *His actual age is 27.*
WARNING: *Actual* often means *present* or *current* in other European languages but this is **very** unusual in English.

Which two of the three words in *italics* have a similar meaning?

....

She is not my *actual* mother, who disappeared when I was three, but at the *present* time she is the only person there is to look after me until I grow up. I have lived in many places during the last three years. My *current* address is 40 The High Street, Greenwich, London, but I will be moving again in a few weeks.

B CONTEXTS

▶ **Read the texts and then decide if the statements which follow are true or false.**

a Present-day Icelandic has changed very little during the last thousand years. In fact, Icelandic people can easily read the stories about their heroes which were written many hundreds of years ago.

The meaning of the words in the Icelandic language is changing very quickly.   **True/False**

b The current expression for a good looking man is 'hunky'.

At the moment it is popular to use 'hunky' for a good looking man but this expression will probably change in a few years.   **True/False**

c Many people in Vilcamba, Ecuador, say they are 120 years old or older but none of them can prove it with an actual birth certificate.

The oldest people of Vilcamba don't have birth certificates.   **True/False**

C PRONUNCIATION

a Does the *u* in *current* have the same pronunciation as the *u* in *cut* or the *oo* in *wood*? ....

b Where is the stress in the words *current* and *present*, the first or second syllable?
....

c Match the word with the correct stress pattern.

actual   i) ☐☐   ii) ☐☐

D WHAT COMES AFTER THE WORD?

GENERAL RULE

| present/ actual | can only be used *before* the noun with the meanings in this unit
Example: *The present generation prefers pop.*
The actual sales are higher than we expected. |

E CHECKING

▶ **Read the sentences and correct the words in *italics* if they are wrong.**

Remember, in many cases both *current* and *present* can be used in the same situation, but when it is clear that change is very quick and expected then *current* is the only choice.

a What is *present* today, is old tomorrow.
b The *present* issue of the magazine has a photo of nomads in the Sahara Desert.
c The *present* leader of Nigeria has another four years in office.
d The *current* exchange rate is $2 to £1.
e The *present*-day language of Iceland has not changed a lot during the last thousand years.
f Have you heard the *present* news about the terrible bush fires in Australia?
g I thought I had £100 in my account but the *present* amount is £50.
h I don't know his *actual* height but he must he about 1.80 metres. But I do know he is shorter than his *actual* girlfriend who he has been dating for only two weeks, which is a long time for him.

F TESTING

▶ **Answer the following questions.**

a Who would probably say 'My current husband is much younger than me'?
  i) a film star who has had many husbands
  ii) somebody who has been married for many years
b What do you think would be the best name for a bank account which you can withdraw money from by cheque at any time?
  i) a current account
  ii) a present account
c What is the correct name for the type of TV programme that discusses the daily changes in politics and finance?
  i) present affairs programme
  ii) current affairs programme
d Does *actual* mean *real*, *present* or *current* in the following sentence?
  The actual financial situation in many countries ten years ago was probably better than today's situation.

G PRACTICE

▶ **Rewrite the sentences without changing the original meaning. Include one of the words in the box in each sentence.**

actual present current

a According to today's bank balance you only have $100.

Your ....

b You mustn't buy it in the condition it's in at the moment,

You mustn't ....

c What is the real meaning of *denouement*?

Do you know .... ?

d I really like to know what is happening in politics and business at the moment.

I'm very interested ....

e Whose is this week's issue of Business News?

Who does the .... ?

Revision E

units 21–25

1 alive, life, live, lively (unit 21)

▶ Write five sentences using all the words in the table. You must use one of the words underlined in each sentence.

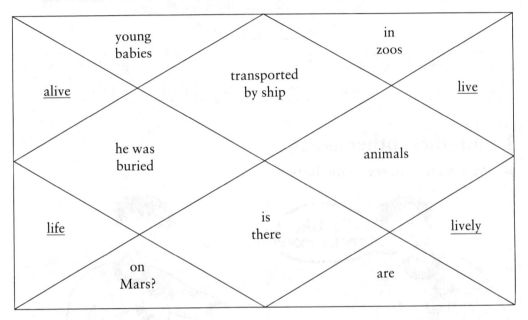

Example: _Animals are lively._

a ....

b ....

c ....

d ....

e ....

2   dead, death, die, died (unit 22)

▶   Which of the four squares fits in the centre of the circle to give four correct sentences? ....

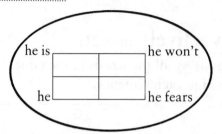

a	die	death	**b**	death	die	**c**	dead	die	**d**	dead	die
	dead	died		died	dead		death	died		died	death

3   another, other (unit 23)

▶   Match the sentences with the pictures

1

2

3

4

a He wants another.

b He wants the other.

c He wants some others.

d He wants the others.

4 during, for, since, while (unit 24)

▶ In which group are all eight combinations correct—*a, b* or *c*?

a

a day ages			a week the night
	for	during	
	while	since	
waiting I was waiting			last night three months

b

then a week			he was ill last week
	since	while	
	during	for	
I was asleep three hours			five hours two days ago

c

waiting I was waiting			three months five hours
	while	for	
	since	during	
I was asleep last night			the night my career

5 actual, current, present (unit 25)

▶ Which group has three correct sentences—*a, b* or *c*?

a I haven't seen the actual ...   Taj Mahal but I've seen a model in a museum.
President because he is on holiday at the moment.
Queen but I saw the previous one.

b The current ...   issue of the magazine is sold out.
team captain is not very popular.
account you opened in our bank has £40 in it.

c The present ...   issue of the magazine is sold out.
team captain is not very popular.
account you opened in our bank has £40 in it.

Answer Key

Unit 1

A a Yes
 b No

B 1 a lend
 b borrow
 2 a Yes
 b No

C 1 All the structures are possible except *a* which should be *lend something to somebody.*

D

infinitive	past simple	past participle
lend	lent	lent
borrow	borrowed	borrowed

E 1a   2b   3b   4b   5b

F 1 a borrowed
 b from
 2 a lends
 b to
 3 a borrowed
 b borrow
 c from

G 1 a Students borrow books from libraries.
 b Rich art collectors lend paintings to galleries.
 c House buyers borrow money from banks.
 d Banks lend money to new businesses.
 2 *Possible answers*
 a ... I will have to borrow one./... who can lend me one?
 b ... lend it to anyone./... let anyone else borrow it.

Unit 2

A 1b   2c   3a

B

infinitive	*-ing* form	past simple	past participle
lie	lying	lay	lain
lie	lying	lied	lied
lay	laying	laid	laid

C 1 a lying
 b lying
 c correct

D 1 a lie
    b lay
    c lying
    d lay
  2 a She lay on the beach and got sunburnt.
    b She laid her towel on the beach because the sand was wet.
    c She lied about the beach—it wasn't sandy at all.

E 1 *Possible answers*
    a ... why don't you lie down?
    b ... can you lay them on the table?
    c ... don't lie about anything.
  2 a He always lied.
    b She laid the table.
    c He lay in bed for an extra hour.

Unit 3

A 1b   2d   3a   4c

B a True
  b True
  c False

C 1 a ii)
    b ii)
  2 True

D 1 a Yes
    b Yes
  2 a This photo reminds me of your father ...
    b Remind me to get ... *or* Remember to get ...
    c I remember taking the money but I don't remember spending it.
    d correct
    e Please remember to switch on ...
  3 a i)
    b ii)
  4 a remember
    b remember
    c reminds

E 1 a He reminded me to visit my friend.
    b He remembered visiting my friend/me.
    c He reminded me of my friend.
    d He remembered to visit my friend/me.
  2 a Jenny reminded Dave to water the plants.
    b The witness remembered seeing someone near the station.
    c Eddie didn't remember to turn off the gas cooker.
    d The sea reminds James Reeves of a hungry dog.

Unit 4

A the fifth person

B 1 *b* is correct
   2 *e* is correct

C red

E a Somebody told me that you would come. *or* Somebody said that you would come.
   c Can you tell me the answer?
   d Can you tell me the answer?
   f Can you tell me the answer?
   g He told me that there were no answers.
   h Somebody told me that you were here. *or* Somebody said that you were here.
   j Can you tell me the answer?
   l He said goodbye to me.
   n He told a long story.

F 1 He said nothing.
   2 He said nothing to him.
   3 He said nothing to his mother.
   4 He said that he was French.
   5 He said a lot.
   6 Don't say anything (please).
   7 Don't tell him.
   8 Don't tell him that he was French.
   9 Don't tell him to write to his mother.
  10 Don't tell him that.

G a I didn't tell the truth.
   b I didn't say anything.
   c I told him to do it again.
   d He said that the new system is no good.
   e I told him the whole message again.
   f I said something about the new company to him.

Unit 5

A 1 a miss   b lose   c waste
   2 a ... your cheque book in the street.
     b ... your time watching TV if you're tired.
     c ... your time watching TV if you're tired.
     d ... your time watching TV if you're tired.
       ... your driving test if you're careful.

B a People spend two hours in their cars every morning travelling to work.
   b Most of the time is wasted sitting in traffic jams.
   c People miss many business appointments because they are late for work.

C news

D *line 1* spend
  line 1 correct
  line 2 waste
  line 2 spend
  line 3 correct
  line 5 missing
  line 7 lose

E **a** missed
  b lost, spent, wasted
  c spent
  d missed
  e miss

F *Possible answers*
  a ... miss it.
  b ... lose it.
  c ... spend all your money.
  d ... miss it.
  e ... waste it.

Revision Unit A

1 A **a** Brian
    b Jenny
    c £15
  B **b** lend something to someone
    c borrow something from someone
  C **a** Can you lend me the money?/Can you lend the money to me?
    b Can I borrow the money from you?

2

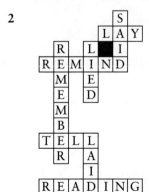

3 A **1** **a** i) No   ii) Yes   iii) Yes
      b i) Yes   ii) No
      c i) Yes   ii) No
      d i) Yes   ii) No
      e i) No   ii) Yes   iii) spent
      f i) Yes   ii) No

2 **a** How did you lose your money? I left it in a bag on the train.

   b How did you waste your money? I bought a theatre ticket and was too ill to go.

   c How did you spend your money? I bought my wife a present.

B **a** He misses gardening because he lives in a flat now.

   b She missed the 6 o'clock train.

   c He wasted a free afternoon going to the zoo.

   d She spends her free time going to the cinema.

   e He had an hour to wait so he passed the time reading a newspaper.

   f She passed the spelling test.

   g She lost her ring when she was washing her hands.

Unit 6

A 1

	object possible	things	people	buildings	vehicles
a	✓		✓		
b	✓		✓	✓	
c	✓			✓	
d					
e	✓	✓ eg a safe		✓	✓

2 **a** mugger

   b thief

   c robber

   d burglar

B Most crimes are committed against property.

D **a** *line 1* Clever criminals do not rob banks ...

   b *line 1* A: Did they steal your car?

E **1** **b** 1, 2, 3, 4, 5

      c 8

      d 1

      e 3, 8, 10

      f 9

F *Possible answers*

   a Thieves stole gold, platinum and diamonds from Heathrow airport.

   b Criminals broke into the Prince's house and took valuable jewellery.

   c A 15-year-old mugged a woman and took her handbag.

   d While robbers were trying to rob a bank, someone took their car.

   e A thief who tried to burgle a villa couldn't leave because of the dog.

Unit 7

A 1c   2b   3a

B **1** 1 Mesomorph   2 Endomorph   3 Ectomorph

2 a True
  b True
  c True

C boot

E a ... do not match
  b correct
  c ... police description does not fit him.

F a match
  b suit
  c fit

G *Possible answers*
  a The clothes suit him because he is a clown.
  b The designs on the trouser legs don't match.
  c His right shoe doesn't fit him.

Unit 8

A

	public	private
a		✓
b		✓
c	✓	
d	✓	✓
e	✓	✓
f	✓	

B a tram
  b BMW motorcycle
  c cable car
  d private car
  e taxi
  f hovercraft

C a *i* in *fight*
  b i)

E *line 2* go in a/by taxi
  line 2 correct
  line 4 take a/get a/go by bus
  line 6 correct
  line 7 travelling by donkey
  line 8 riding a bike
  line 8 correct

F a a donkey
  b a donkey, the tube, the coach, a plane, the ferry
  c a taxi, a car (the coach, a plane—if used for private transport)

    d donkey, tube, taxi, car, coach, plane, ferry
    e a donkey, the tube, a taxi, a car, the coach, a plane, the ferry
    f the tube, a taxi, the coach, a plane, the ferry

G *Possible answers*
    a ... get a train to work.
    b ... ride a bicycle to work.
    c ... go to work in your boss's car.
    d ... take a taxi to work.
    e ... travel by plane.
    f ... drive a tractor.

Unit 9

A **1** **a** What did you hear? A sudden noise.
      b What did you listen to? My favourite cassette for half an hour.
  2 *b* is not logical.

B Yes

C **a** *t*
   b near

E **a** correct
   b ... I wasn't listening.
   c correct
   d ... I have ever heard.
   e Listen to the sound ...
   f correct

F **a** I can't hear her voice—it's too quiet.
   b I can't listen to her voice—it's so awful.
   c Please listen carefully—it's important.
   d Please listen to her voice—it's wonderful.

G *Possible answers*
    a ... can't hear.
    b ... don't listen.
    c ... hear.
    d ... listen.
    e ... hear properly.
    f ... listen.
    g ... listen to it.

Unit 10

A **a** Did you look at his tie? It had an unusual design.
   b Did you see his tie? It was his birthday present.
   c Did you watch his tie? It was moving—he's a magician.

B If the pupils in their eyes become larger, it means they like you.

D **a** correct
 b correct
 c If you look at the face ...   correct
 d correct
 e Look at the video ...
 f correct
 g Don't watch!   correct

E **a** Can you see the TV? Oh no! Somebody has stolen it.
 b Can you watch TV? Yes, but only for an hour.
 c Look at the TV. Oh no! It's scratched.

F *Possible answers*
 a ... can't see them clearly.
 b ... look carefully.
 c ... look at ...
 d ... watch.

Revision Unit B

1 A **a** broke into
 b rob
 c breaking into/burgling
 d broke into/burgled, stolen
 e mug
 f broke in

2 A **a** Do the shoes fit you? No, they're too big.
 b Do the shoes match? No, one's a darker green than the other.
 c Do the shoes suit you? No, green looks terrible on me.

3 A **a** by car
 b in a concert hall

 B **1** **a** i)
 b iii)
 c ii)
 2 **a** iii)
 b iii)
 c i)

 C **a** go
 b drove
 c take/get
 d take/get

4 **1** In June 1950, 30 million adults switched on their radios to listen to a boxing match but at first all they were able to hear was the sound of an electric storm.
 2 'Listen, can you hear anything?'
 'Yes.'
 'Good. Now listen to Handel's music.'

5 **a** Can you look and try to find my socks?
   b Can you look at the sun without hurting your eyes?
   c Can you see anything in the dark?
   d Can you watch the race on TV at 3 o'clock?

Unit 11

A **a** coming
   b going

B **1**

	Is the speaker at the prison?	Is the listener at the prison?
a		
b		✓
c	✓	
d	✓	✓

   2 True

C **a** some, run, done
   b no, so

E **a** False
   b False

F **1** **a** No
      b go
      c go
   2 **a** goes
      b comes

G *Possible answers*
   a ... come here to watch it?
   b ... go to his house.

Unit 12

A Scientists invented the computer.

B **a** No
   b It was taken in Asia.
   c The public couldn't see the photo in London because it didn't exist.
   d False

C **1** **a** ii)
      b i)
   2 *o* in *other*

D **1** **a** invented
      b discovered
      c invented
      d invented

2 a invent
  b discover

E *Possible answers*
  a On Easter Day 1772, Jacob Roggeveen discovered Easter Island with its strange statues called 'moais'.
  b Karl Benz invented the first car in 1885.

Unit 13

A a bring
  b get/bring
  c taking
  d get
  e take

B

infinitive	past simple	past participle
get	got	got
take	took	taken
bring	brought	brought

C a the Yanomami Indians
  b No
  c i) Yes
    ii) Yes

D a ... I'll take you in my car.
  b correct
  c ... didn't bring us ...
  d correct
  e Can you take the coffee ...
  f Can you get the coffee ...

E a bring
  b take
  c take, bring
  d take, bring, get

F *Possible answers*
  1 ... get the fire extinguisher.
  2 ... can you take it to him please?
  3 ... can you bring the spare key round please?

Unit 14

A b 2, 6, 7   c 1, 3, 5

B True

C	object	no object
a	✓	
b		✓
c		✓
d	✓	
e		✓
f	✓	

D a pear
  b *t* in *to*

E 1 b Let me dress in/put on my new clothes.
  d Let me take off my old jeans ...
  g Do you like what I've got on?
  j Shall I take my new bag?
 2 a dress
  b is wearing
  c put ... on
  d getting dressed
  e is ... dressed, take off
  f has got ... on

F *Possible answers*
 1 You should not have a hat on when you enter a church.
 2 You should put on warm clothes in cold weather.
 3 You should wear a mask at the carnival in Venice.
 4 You should take your shoes off when you go into a house in Japan.
 5 You should be dressed in white when you get married.
 6 You should get dressed quickly in the morning.

Unit 15

A a eyes
  b after you check it
  c your mother
  d ii)

B 1 the customer
 2 a Yes
  b The blood/the cut on the customer's head.
  c The customer's limp when he came in.
  d After he had looked carefully at the customer's condition.

C a i)   **b** i)   **c** ii)   **d** i)

D **1** **b** 2   **c** 2, 3, 4   **d** 1, 5
   2 3

E **1** **a** recognise
     b notice
     c realise
     d remark
   2 **a** Do you realise ...
     b I did not notice the soldiers ...
     c correct

F **a** Yes, I recognised the man from the train.
   b When I noticed that he had a gun.
   c Yes, I remarked on the weather.
   d Not when I realised that he was pointing the gun at himself.

Revision Unit C

1 1b   2a
2 There is a theory that somebody invented the aeroplane 500 years ago and then hid the plans which were never discovered.
3 **1** I'll get the flowers.
   2 I'll take the chocolates.
   3 I'll bring the bread.
4 **a** put on, take off
   b recognise
   c realise
   d remark on
   e remark
   f i) notice
     ii) Is ... dressed, has ... got ... on
     iii) get dressed
     iv) dress
     v) wore

Unit 16

A **a** check, examine
   b test
   c control

B **1** c
   2 **a** False
     b True
     c i) True
        ii) True

C **1** **a** i)
     b ii)
   2 win

D *line 1* check
 line 2 correct
 line 4 correct
 line 5 control
 line 6 correct

E *Possible answers*
 a ... control your eyesight.
 b ... examining your eyes.
 c ... test your eyes.
 d ... check your eyes.

Unit 17

A *a* is about sport

B The sport is called Sepak Takrow.
 The description matches the picture.

C *a* in *cat*

E *line 1* game
 line 2 game
 line 3 game
 line 4 correct
 line 5 correct
 line 6 correct

F 1c   2a   3b

G *Possible answers*
 a Did you see the match last night?
 b Have you ever played the game of squash?
 c Wasn't that fantastic play?

Unit 18

A **a** travel, journey, trip, excursion
 b travel

B Text **a** is about the longest distance
 Text **c** is about the shortest distance

C

	long short distance		only short time at destination	pleasure	serious	land	sea/ air/ space
a	✓				✓		✓
b	✓	✓		✓	✓	✓	✓
c		✓	✓	✓		✓	✓
d	✓	✓		✓	✓	✓	✓

D **1** fridge

  2 **a** ii)

    b ii)

    c ii)

    d ii)

E **a** Correct

  b Correct

  c Incorrect

  d Incorrect—you have to use the verb *travel*

F **1** **a** down the river

    b to the South Seas   *voyage*

    c to the stars

  2 **a** down the river

    b across the Kalahari desert

    c along the old Silk Road from China to Europe   *journey*

    d to the South Seas

    e to the stars

  3 **a** down the river

    b half day   *excursion*

    c sightseeing

  4 **a** down the river

    b across the Kalahari desert

    c along the old Silk Road from China to Europe

    d to the stars   *trip*

    e to the South Seas

    f sightseeing

    g half day

    h business

G *Possible answers*

  1 In 1770, Captain Cook made/went on a voyage to Australia.

  2 There is an excursion to Cambridge on Saturday.

  3 William Shaw has gone on a business trip to Tokyo.

  4 How long is the journey from London to Paris?

  5 Travel ...

Unit 19

A **a** Sorry?/Pardon?

  b Please sit down.

  c Sorry!

  d Excuse me.

  e Here you are./There you are.

  f Yes, please.

B **a** No, only the last one is successful.

  b No

  c True

C 1 a the first syllable
    b the second syllable
    c the first syllable
  2 Here, are
  3 True
  4 a i) a request to repeat
      ii) an apology
    b The voice rises in the question.

D *line 1*   Sorry.
   line 4   Please
   line 6   correct
   line 7   correct
   line 8   correct
   line 10 Here you are./There you are.
   line 12 Excuse me!
   line 13 Excuse me
   line 14 correct

E 1 Sorry!
  2 Here you are.
  3 Pardon?
  4 please.
  5 Excuse me.

Unit 20

A 1 a exciting
    b interesting
    c bored
    d excited
    e interested
    f boring
  2 a *-ing*
    b *-ed*
    c *-ing*
    d *-ed*

B a False
  b False
  c True
  d True
  e True
  f True

C 1 a three
    b one
    c three
  2 a on the first syllable
    b on the second syllable

E   **a**   I'm very interested in ...
      b   ... because I was bored.
      c   I would be very interested in going ...
      d   I am very excited about ...

F   2d   3a   4c   5f   6e

G   *Possible answers*
      a   ... do you find the most boring?
      b   ... in the race do you feel the most excited?
      c   ... part of the season do you find the most interesting?

Revision Unit D

1   **1**   ... you check his passport ...
      2   correct
      3   ... to check the plane's lights ...
      4   correct
      5   Who will check/control the number ...
      6   correct

2   2, 5, 9   3, 8, 11   4, 6, 12

3   **2**

2	trip	for pleasure/business short time at destination	two days in Tokyo
3	excursion	short, for pleasure in a group, return same day, on a coach or boat	a full day on the river
4	journey	general word—interested in time/distance	five miles to work takes 20 minutes
5	travel	abstract noun	through the Americas on horseback

4   b, h, f, e, d, g, a, c

5   **a**   It is easier to be interested in politics than to be interested in politicians.
      b   I am more interested in film stars because I find them more exciting.

Unit 21

A   **1**   live
      2   lively
      3   alive

B   **a**   an old and experienced person
      b   a depressed person
      c   the sheriff in an American Western
      d   a radio announcer
      e   a man in love

C	with	side
a		✓
b	✓	
c		✓
d		✓
e		✓
f	✓	

D 1 a My lively grandmother ...
  b ... is still alive ...
  c ... between life and death?
  d ... we do not know if we are alive or dead.
  2 a i) The TV show will be happening at the same time as it is broadcast.
    ii) There will be a lot of action on the show.
  b i) They hadn't died when I arrived.
    ii) They hadn't moved house.

E a live
  b alive
  c life
  d live
  e lively

F *Possible answers*
  a ... the life of a minke whale long?
  b ... will the minke whale live?
  c ... minke whales lively?
  d ... the programme live?
  e ... the whale still alive?

Unit 22

A a Yes
  b Four—do, drink, drive, die
  c The lifestyle of the man had nothing to do with the insurance company.

B a head
  b breath

C a to be dead
  b to die

D die—live
  death—life
  died—lived

E 1 a When did the dinosaur die?
  b correct
  c The dinosaur has been dead for ...

    d The dinosaur has already died.
    e correct
    f correct
    g The dinosaur died ...
    h correct
  2 a There is no pain like the death of a friend.
    b It is better to die on your feet than to live on your knees.
    c Only dead fish swim with the tide.
    d I hate your ideas but I am ready to die for your right to express them.

F *Possible answers*
  a How long has the dodo been dead?
  b When did the last dodo die?
  c Was the death of the dodo a long time ago?

Unit 23

A

	singular	plural	definite	indefinitive
a others		✓		✓
b the other	✓		✓	
c the others		✓	✓	

B **a** False
  b False
  c False
  d True

C **1 a** True
    b True
  2 a Show him another coat.
    Show him another one.
    Show him another.
    b Let her see the other dresses.
    Let her see the other ones.
    Let her see the others.
    c Have you got any other hats?
    Have you got any other ones?
    Have you got any others?
    d I prefer the other suit.
    I prefer the other one.
    I prefer the other.

D **a** ... give me another one?
  b ... I can show you the others.
  c ... others find it too difficult.
  d ... Another way is to use ...
  e correct

E 1 *o* in *son*
   2 a ii)
     b i)
     c i)

F a the other
  b other
  c another
  d others
  e the others

G *Possible answers*
  a ... not the other.
  b ... give me another?
  c ... the others to do.
  d ... others don't.

Unit 24

A a Monday, that moment, 3 pm, last year, he was outside, February, then, watching TV, the storm, yesterday
  b 24 hours, most of the year, six days, a long time, ages, a fortnight
  c last year, February, the storm, those nine months
  d he was outside, watching TV, the others were sleeping

B a we do not know
  b during the last hour
  c a minute ago

C a *i* in *sing*
  b *i* in *mile*
  c ii)

D a ... for a few weeks.
  b correct
  c ... while it was on the ship.
  d ... the mast for/during the whole trip.
  e correct
  f correct
  g correct

E a The security camera was/has been on for 9 hours.
  b The security camera was on during the bank robbery.
  c The security camera has been on since 9 o'clock.
  d The security camera was on while the robbers were in the bank.

F a Chinese has been used for 3000 years or more.
  b Bones have been found which show that Chinese characters have been used since 1123 BC.
  c Chinese children use 'pinyin' while they are learning the more complicated characters.
  d During Mao Tse-Tung's time the more complicated characters were simplified.

Unit 25

A a present, current

B a False
   b True,
   c True

C a *u* in *cut*
   b the first syllable
   c i)

E a What is current today ...
   b The current issue ...
   c correct
   d correct
   e correct
   f ... the current news ...
   g ... the actual amount was £50.
   h correct, ... is shorter than his current girlfriend ...

F a i)
   b i)
   c ii)
   d real

G *Possible answers*
   a Your current account has only $100 in it.
   b You mustn't buy it in its present condition.
   c Do you know the actual meaning of *denouement*?
   d I'm very interested in current affairs.
   e Who does the current issue of Business News belong to?

Revision Unit E

1 a Live animals are transported by ship.
   b Young babies are lively.
   c Is there life on Mars?
   d He was buried alive.
   e Animals live in zoos.

2 d

3 1c   2a   3d   4b

4 c

5 b

Index

The numbers in this Index refers to units.